The Art of Riding Smooth

Plus: The Best 2000 Mile Route You'll Ever Ride!

By
Jim Ford

Copyright © 2017 Jim Ford

*In every endeavor, amidst the multitudes,
there are those who embrace it, truly.* Jeff Hughes

Acknowledgements

There is no way this book would have been completed without the guidance from these three individuals: Wendy Crosby, Michael Dale, and my sweet Annie Hayes. My heartfelt appreciation goes to each of you.

And there were others: I owe a debt of gratitude to the following individuals as well who, in their special way both large and small, contributed to the inspiration of this book:

Ed Abbott, Michael Abraham, Mary Baker, Steve Barone, Will Beers, Paul Binder, David Bliss, Tom Buzas, Ken D'Arcy, Art and Lyn Etling, Ron Feurer, Amanda Ford, Jim Gebhardt, Jennings Glenn, Jonathan Graham, Jay Grosse, Bob Henig, Dan Kauffman, Moshe Levy, Kaili Mang, Roy and Marie Morris, Jim Parks, Peter Perrin, Ed Read, Peter Rockwood, Walton Rogers, Sim Savage, Jim Shaw, Mike Shepherd, Phil Sulfstede, Tim Sundgren, Mark Tichenor, and Doug Waines.

Thank you!

Cap'n Rick in 2006

I'd like to dedicate these pages to Richard Norton, CFII (1946-2009.) My friend, Rick, taught me the art of instrument flying. In so doing, he also taught me how to teach.

Table of Contents

Introduction 1

A Bit of Background 5

Basic Seating on a Sport-Touring Motorcycle 19

Reading the Road Part 1 24

Reading the Road Part 2 34

Reading the Road Part 3 44

It's All About Curves 58

Leaning a Motorcycle 79

Managing the Engine and Momentum 90

The Art of Riding Smooth 119

The Magical Mountainous Tour 122

Introduction

A reassuring vibration thrums beneath me as I roll north and away from the sun. It's late afternoon. The mountain landscape, occasionally backlit by shafts of brilliant autumn-amber sunlight, streams by in a satisfying blur. Recent rain grudgingly moves off to the southwest and when I turn my eyes away from the task at hand, I make out a nascent rainbow. A layer of broken blue hovers above, yet just ahead, ghostly gray billows and lifts off the pavement. Murk momentarily engulfs me. Almost immediately I burst back into sudden clear air. More fog ahead. More blue high up in the distance. Spray from my spinning wheels diminishes as traction improves from wet to damp to dry along this Holy Grail of East Coast mountain roads—the fabulous Blue Ridge Parkway. I love it. The sights. The sounds. The speed. I love it all, fiercely. Farther along, as shadows elongate, I nod while banking into the hundredth curve. This *is* just like flying—only on a motorcycle!

* * *

Acquaintances comment how curious it is that I ride one. I tell them I own and ride two. "But isn't it

INTRODUCTION

dangerous?" they ask. "No," I tell them, "not really, but then I'm trained to ride." I explain that motorcycling is my passion, although I rarely explain how deep the passion goes. They would never fully understand. I am reminded of a recent ad for our local newspaper pronouncing: "If you don't get it, you won't get it." That sums up one-half of the coin: Unless a person buys a motorcycle and learns to ride, that person will never fully understand why we who ride—ride.

But how about the other half of the coin? Might you, dear reader, presently holding this book, also embrace the joy of riding a motorcycle? If you do, how does the idea of insanely great motorcycling stoke you? I hope so, since that's how it has been for me all these years. The reason is simple: I am meant to ride! *I am* a rider. How about you? Are you also meant to ride? Do you feel a deep passion for motorcycling too?

The first time I rode a motorcycle, it was as if I already knew how. I didn't have to be shown much at all. I suppose I would be called intuitive when it comes to riding. I'm a natural for knowing roads too. If you're an intuitive rider like me and know your roads, that's great; you'll still find this book interesting. But if you are not quite like me; if you're not an intuitive rider, or feel you're not quite as good or as confident as you'd like to be, or just want to know some excellent roads, then what is written on these pages will be of great interest to you. That's because, intuitive or not, this book is written for riders who are passionate about motorcycling and want to take their skills to the next level. If you are determined to get better at the *craft* of motorcycling, and then want to get out there and ride some amazing roads, this book is definitely for you!

The journey to mastery goes something like this: Initially, a beginner student is "unconsciously incompetent," meaning the student has an inborn interest but has no concept of what the skills are. With a little practice, the new student becomes a novice. The novice is "consciously incompetent," meaning he or she is still not competent and knows it, so is going about learning and obtaining the skills required to get better. Having obtained these skills by *regular practice with the earnest intent to get better,* the novice becomes a journeyman. The journeyman is "consciously competent," meaning he or she has developed skills and has become pretty good—but not great. The journeyman has to be constantly conscious of what he or she is doing and why. Finally mastery is achieved. A master is "unconsciously competent," meaning she or he is expert at what they do without having to think about it.

This book will take you from the second level to the third level. Developing the fourth level is up to you, but it's where the action is. Luckily, mastery is not too difficult to achieve either if passion is your propellent. Masters no longer have to think about fundamental skills. They have absorbed them; they *are* those skills. This freedom allows them to be creative, bending and even breaking the rules if they like, using the skills they have embodied. The fourth level is also where the "art" of one's passion resides. No telling where your motorcycling mastery will take you. But you can count on your experiences being thrilling, life affirming, and sometimes quite transcendent. There's just nothing else in motorsports like it.

At age 40, I bought a motorcycle and began my journey toward the next level and the next. Twenty-five years and several hundred thousand miles later, I'd like to share what I've learned. It's my hope that the information contained on these pages will fortify you with ability and confidence—like a booster-shot for both the mind and spirit!

* * *

My final chapter is a description of the best 2,000 mile curvy road route you'll ever ride! That's because the route is through a region that serves up the most miles of nearly continuous hilly, twisty roads found anywhere in the United States and perhaps the world: The Appalachian Mountains.

You now know what I intend to do. In return, all I ask you to do is keep an open mind.

A Bit of Background...

Invariably, at some point during one of my one-or two-day motorcycling workshops known as The Rider's Workshop, at least one participant will make the suggestion: "Jim, you must write a book!" My reply has always been, "Maybe someday."

I've said "maybe" all these years because a glance through any online bookstore reveals nearly a dozen volumes on motorcycle riding that are informative and well-written. With all this useful information, I asked myself if I really had anything new to add.

An instructor's life experience infuses the content and quality of his or her curriculum. Skimming through these books, it seemed as if a large part of each author's riding experience came from racetrack competition or from the excellent Motorcycle Safety Foundation curriculum. The more I thought about it, the more I realized that certain aspects of my life experience do enable me to add some new information, or at least add more insight to the ever-growing body of knowledge of motorcycling skills.

Two pursuits have shaped my approach to writing this book: First, being a licensed pilot, and second, by having led Appalachian Mountain motorcycle workshops and tours professionally for the past 11 years. Having been mentored as well in my early years of motorcycling by one of the most complete motorcyclists ever adds a third, and crucially formative, dimension to my riding and coaching.

Here's the takeaway: While airplanes and motorcycles obviously differ, the mindset to expertly operate each is essentially the same. Both require continuous anticipation, precision, and smoothness. Anticipation, precision, and smoothness are my "thing." And, in my Rider's Workshop, my approach has been to explain, demonstrate, and then coach riders on how to "fly" their motorcycle with these three skills continuously in mind.

***

My father was highly trained in his work, so whatever my interests were as a kid, he'd urge me to seek any possible training first. "Why?" I'd ask. "To benefit from organized knowledge, structured supervision, and to develop good habits," he'd reply. My father knew there was no specific motorcycle rider safety training available at the time. It hadn't yet been invented. He also knew that riding a motorcycle was doable without training, but not very safe. He therefore decreed that I was not to ride a motorcycle as long as I lived under his roof. Being an obedient son, I never did. What he did encourage, however, was for me to do what he once did: Earn my pilot's license because learning to fly an airplane did require extensive training, much of it pertaining to safety. I became a pilot, developed safe habits, and wound up flying extensively for twenty years. Initially, my flying opportunities were limited to clear atmosphere because my training was basic. Eventually I put myself through additional training and earned my instrument certificate. The ability to navigate a flight entirely by reference to flight instruments gave me the freedom to fly whenever I chose. The weather could be clear or cloudy, stormy or bright—it didn't matter. In later years, utilizing those skills and training, I ferried ambulatory patients up and down the East Coast for a charity organization called Angel Flight. Charity flying gave me a lot of experience flying in all kinds of weather. I'll describe a pivotal 'Angel Flight' a little later on.

By and by, flying no longer seemed to interest me the way it once did. I had taken control of my airplane to a high level. My tolerance for error was routinely limited to the width of the instrument needles themselves. Frankly, there just weren't many single-engine flying challenges left for me without investing a lot more dough. Then, one day I read that operating motorcycles and airplanes had much in common. Oh boy! *That* piqued my interest. By this time, I was in my late thirties and had never once ridden a motorcycle, so the thought that maybe it wasn't too late to learn struck me like a thunderbolt! I was to rediscover something that had fascinated me as a kid and apparently had qualities similar to flying—motorcycling! Almost immediately I took the state-prescribed safety course, passed the written and riding tests with flying colors (pun intended) and purchased my first motorcycle—all during the week of my 40th birthday. I soon came to find motorcycling so mesmerizing and so natural that I determined to change careers. In 1996, I closed the door on a prosperous career in the insurance industry, and joined a prominent Maryland motorcycle dealership in motorcycle sales—earning half my previous income. Happily, the "motorcycling life" has been my vocation ever since.

Paul Mihalka with the author in 2000

In those early years, the dealership had just two salesmen—Paul Mihalka and myself.

"When the student is ready, the teacher appears," so the saying goes. It surely describes my relationship with Paul during my years as a journeyman rider. I came to learn that Paul (who sadly died of a sudden illness in 2013) was a master motorcyclist. According to his annual mileage log, he had accumulated over 1,400,000 lifetime miles: 400,000 in South America and over 1 million in the US. But it wasn't just miles that he had accumulated; it was his entire persona. He had a worldly aura. He was born in Hungary before the Second World War. His father, a Hungarian military officer, fled with his young family to Venezuela just as the Red Army descended upon Budapest. It was there, in Caracas, that Paul grew up, eventually developing into a motorcyclist and ultimately into a bit of a legend.

I knew Paul was a bit of a sage as well when I complained early on in my tenure about our paltry income compared to many of the customers who walked through the door. "That's true," he said. Then he looked at me and with a wink asked, "But who has more fun?" "Aha!" I thought, grinning large. Thereafter, I was all in! Ours was the beginning of a beautiful friendship.

A Bit of Background...

"Pablo" sometime during the mid-1950s

The 1950s was a period when motorcycle racing was still in its infancy. In those years, many motorcyclists never even finished a race because their machines routinely broke down. Paul, then in his twenties, became renowned for finishing every race he started. He eventually went on to become a two-time Venezuelan and a one-time All-South-American race champion in what was the largest engine class of the time. Throughout South America, he was commonly known in racing circles and beyond as "Pablo" such was the extent of his fame. From those years to nearly the day of his death, he was riding motorcycles. Paul personified motorcycling from its early stages right on up into the modern era. He lived its ethos and shared his experiences and knowledge with me in his distinctive Germanic accent. He was a master. I was his protégé—and, like a sponge, I soaked it up.

* * *

One Sunday morning we decided to meet for brunch at a favorite haunt of mine south of Front Royal, Virginia. Arranging this get-together took some selling on my part because by that time of morning, Paul would normally have been well on the back half of his routine Sunday ride. After our brunch he suggested we go for what he termed a "little ride." "Sure," I said. "No problem." I thought we'd simply angle back easterly toward home and maybe he'd show me a new road or two on the way home. Instead, we swung westward, accelerated up and over the Blue Ridge and straight across the Shenandoah Valley. Watching Paul motor up and over that first ridge at Thornton Gap was, for me, like Keith Richards hearing a Chuck Berry lick for the first time. POW!

A Bit of Background...

From The Shenandoah, we headed even farther west, up and over another ridge line and finally into the Appalachians. As we swept northbound along a winding, largely deserted valley road, it dawned on me that I was on a ride like none before. This was strikingly fresh territory for me, with new roads, new scenery and a spanking new skill level required just to keep up! Paul rolled on the throttle and laid down a sinuous, spirited groove for a satisfying number of miles. Never overly fast on the straights or in the curves, his style was effortlessly smooth. We shared a brief stop to gas up, knocked back a hot chocolate, and shared a laugh before we headed even deeper into mountains farther north. Man, this was FUN! The next thing I knew, I was seeing "city limit" signs for Berkeley Springs, West Virginia. By the time I finally got home, my trip odometer had rung up 370+ miles—just like that.

My concept of motorcycling forever changed that day. My riding radius had been stretched and my motorcycling ability had been stretched even further. That ride was also my introduction to the concept of riding "smooth." Up, down and along all those miles of back roads, neither Paul's speed nor his line wavered much as he demonstrated how artfully it could be done. Before a curve, in one fell swoop, he'd steep-lean his big-bore BMW only to quickly straighten up and pull away in a puff of smoke. His line wasn't so much a line, it was a rock-solid rail! When I asked Paul how he did this, he'd laugh and say, "Jim, I simply love to ride. That's all there is to it. After all these years, I still get a kick out of trying to be smoother. No more."

Paul's effortless riding style was a thing of beauty to my journeyman's eyes. His was the look of sheer effortlessness like a seasoned snow skier swishing down a white slope. It had evolved over decades and had originated at a time when both motorcycles and roads were pretty rudimentary. Those were the days of drum brakes. Drums didn't have nearly the stopping power of modern-day caliper/disc brakes, so engine-braking was the norm on the track as well as the street. Paul emphasized engine-braking, which happens to be conducive to controlling momentum and for producing a look of overall smoothness. Seldom showing any brake lights, and with his "making-it-look-easy," upright riding style, I called him "The Sphinx." It appeared to me that he sat motionless in the saddle. I told him that he looked effortless. He turned and said, "Exactly. That's the look!" His was a world of mountain curves; it was where his artistry resided. Paul's seamlessness seemed telepathic; his anticipation of what lay ahead was PFM (Pure F**king Magic!)

Paul and I worked together for nine years. I never planned to quit selling motorcycles, but my enthusiasm for bike sales eventually waned, and as it did, I felt an overpowering urge within to create something unique and of real value for motorcycle owners who love to ride. I took my flying experience, my riding experience, and in-depth discussions with a former racing champion, and created The Rider's Workshop. I teach a style of advanced motorcycling that mirrors Paul's effortless look. I call it "The Art of Riding Smooth" because that's what you become: Smooth. I've taught the course for 11 years. With this book, I will humbly attempt to contribute to the already large and growing canon of motorcycle knowledge but will here focus on the specific domain of riding twisty mountain roads. If you learn to ride mountains and learn to ride them smoothly, you'll be able to ride any road, anywhere, and ride them all really well.

***

"Why mountain riding?"

First off, mountain riding is a unique genre of motorcycling, just as long-distance Iron Butt riding, track day-riding, trials riding, commuting, cross-country motorcycle touring, and just plain riding around are all unique genres of motorcycling, not to mention the universe of off-pavement motorcycling. Each requires its own particular skill set. To an Iron Butt specialist, riding well might mean developing hard-core riding endurance, efficient routing strategies for maximum point accumulation, and judicious downtime management. To the track-day racer, riding well usually means being the fastest cat on the track. A trials rider is always looking for crazy-cool obstacles to ride in, over, through and across without having to dab his or her feet down. Commuting certainly involves managing traffic and keeping a "ring of security" around the motorcycle at all times emphasizing visibility and conspicuity. Motorcycle touring often involves learning two-up riding techniques, big-bike handling skills, along with knowing how to pack efficiently and how to plan routes with the best cuisine and scenery in mind. Finally, riding around requires no more than that—riding around.

Of the various motorcycling genres, track-day and mountain riding enjoy things both similar and dissimilar. Both are ridden in spectacular environments—but are as different as they are spectacular. A typical racetrack is utterly man-made and for the rider, it's about roaring down wide-open straight-a-ways and steep-leaning through engineered curves—repetitively. Riding mountains is equally thrilling but the polar opposite of the track, since the sport is ridden entirely through natural settings and isn't repetitive at all. Instead, mountain riding is about—change.

The mountains, particularly the Appalachians Mountains, are an environment of continuous asymmetrical curves. There are changes in elevation, changes in momentum, changes in traction, and ever-changing scenery and weather. In fact, one might characterize mountain riding as a "study of change" since nothing in those higher elevations ever seems to stay the same for very long. Mountain riding is also all about freedom. Its joy derives from a cacophony of technical, geological, botanical, and meteorological variety that just can't be found elsewhere!

Both genres are also intrinsically sporting genres, enjoying a common intense mindset of technique perfection but with different end-goals. The goal of a track rider is to achieve the highest possible circuit speed in a very predictable environment while riding on the razor's edge of traction just short of disaster. The mindset of mountain riding is to maximize FUN in a largely unpredictable environment while balancing a judicious application of speed with carefully selected sight-lines, bike placement, and lean-angles with safety continuously in mind.

To ride either environment well, the rider must work toward becoming one with both his motorcycle and the roadway. This fusion begins with the mind being continuously focused on one particular thing: To ride within a *mental structure* specific to the genre. On the track, the mental structure facilitates maximum speed. In the mountains, the mental structure facilitates safety without sacrificing fun. In fact, paradoxically, in the mountains, the mental structure ridden to achieve maximum safety is exactly what creates the maximum fun. It's all about achieving maximum proficiency, which I'll explain in a later chapter but safety is paramount! You see failure on the track is not nearly as dire as it is in the mountains. On the track, the facility has engineered all manner of protective run-off barriers and open fields and has EMT mere minutes away. In the mountains, you have flesh-eating guard rails, traction snatching gravel, shear cliffs, and EMT that may be hours away—if they can even find you. With the stakes so high, there's just no alternative but to focus on maximum safety when riding mountains. I'll describe this vital mental structure in detail in a later chapter but becoming "unconsciously competent" *within* the confines of each structure is what beelines you to riding mastery—no matter what genre you choose to ride.

* * *

It's important to understand that riding within the confines of these structures is what creates the ultimate in FUN on a motorcycle. That's right! It is fun to nail a curve with exacting placement, in the right gear, at the right speed, at the right lean angle, and it is fun to set yourself up all over again for the next curve and the next. And finally, feeling exhilarated gliding over mountain roads with complete confidence and ease *is* fun. If having FUN is the main reason why you ride a motorcycle, then this book is for you. It's written for those wanting to dedicate themselves to the journey toward mastery of riding a sport-touring motorcycle in a mountainous environment.

Finally, and not to sound too mystical, but mountain riding with a high level focus can also repeatedly lead you to a "Zen-like" meditative state. This is because mountain riding holds your focus in the moment. Again, it's how you stay safe and keep from crashing. At some point, your deep focus on safety can actually slip your mind through a portal into a prolonged state of profound stillness. You can ride many, many miles and not know how long it took you to get there. Time and distance appear to compress into a continuous flow of "now." I'll describe later on how to induce this rather euphoric state of being for yourself. It's as if a "Holy Ghost" takes you over!

(NOTE: While I will focus on sport-touring motorcycles, these skills can largely be applied to all makes and models of motorcycles.)

Basic Seating on a Sport-Touring Motorcycle

Truth be known: If you are determined to become a better motorcyclist, you will have to change. You'll change from the motorcyclist you are today into whatever kind of better motorcyclist you aspire to become. But you know the drill: Change isn't easy! Getting better isn't easy either. Both require sincere self assessment and the willingness to give up on bad habits for newer, better ones. Then, if you're wise, it's not a bad idea to seek some training. You'll know the skills after reading a book like this, but you won't *own* them. Training develops ownership.

So, where to start? As a rider, every time you saddle up, you experience changes in inertia and momentum as you accelerate, decelerate, ascend and descend. You feel a range of centrifugal forces as you lean your motorcycle from side to side. You also feel high anxiety, utter euphoria, and every other human emotion in between.

Given the importance of fusing with your motorcycle, and since most riders just sit on a motorcycle without giving much thought to how they sit, there's no better place to start than to consider just that: Improving how you sit on your motor-cycle. It's going to move you toward becoming one with your motorcycle and then with the road.

* * *

Basic seating posture begins with your feet and ends with your hands. So, while sitting on your motorcycle, either on its center-stand or supported by a friend, take a deep breath and sit up straight. Let your arms dangle at your sides. Now slide the balls of your feet back so they are centered squarely on the foot pegs. Sit up straight and gently arch your spine. As you do, take another deep breath through your nose. Then exhale through your mouth and feel the increase in energy or "chi" flow through you. Relax.

With the balls of your feet, not your instep, squarely on the foot pegs, grip the tank firmly with your thighs and henceforth focus on using your thigh muscles as the primary means for hanging onto the motorcycle. Use your core muscles for holding your torso upright. This is not to say that you won't use your hands to hang on. But from now on, emphasize using your leg muscles as the primary gripping force and using your arms and hands more for their control function than for primary support. Any time you feel tense or feel the need to hang on tighter, clench the tank with greater emphasis using your thighs while still keeping your upper body loose. In other words, express your tension with your legs, and force yourself to keep your arms loose.

While still sitting upright with your arms and hands dangling at your sides, imagine your spine and thighs joining to form a 90 degree angle. Relax and lean forward about 30 degree at the crease of your hips, and rest your hands lightly on the handlebars. Lean forward such that your elbows are slightly bent and pointed down. That's the point—bent elbows! As you ride, focus on leaning forward and keeping those elbows bent. Let gravity assist. Let your elbows drop straight down as opposed to splaying them out to the side.

Leaning forward with elbows bent helps keep your forearms loose—almost floppy. This is how relaxed those elbows and forearms need to be. The goal is for your elbows and forearms to remain so loose that they act as upper torso shock-absorbers as you roll over surface irregularities. Let your wrists and hands rest softly on the hand rests while operating the controls. Think "hand rests"—not "hand GRIPS"! This emphasis on softness will give you the best throttle control.

"Soft" hands. When your hands are soft, your awareness magically "extends" from your palms and fingertips through the handlebars and into the inner mechanicals of your motorcycle. Truly feel the machine. If you sit stiffly, balled up and tense, you'll jiggle a lot and just try to hold on. If you sit loosely, you and your bike can motor harmoniously as one.

Basic Seating on a Sport-Touring Motorcycle

Become one with your machine like a mythical centaur.

For a moment, reflect on your other senses. When detecting an aroma, don't your nostrils flare and lightly sniff? When you taste, doesn't your tongue lightly massage whatever crosses your pallet? You sip, not gulp, right? A feathery lightness gives each of your senses the heightened awareness necessary to distinguish the important characteristics you're trying to discern. Your sense of touch is no different.

Think of the hand rests as if they were delicate eggshells. Handle your hand-rests that softly. Feel the mechanical "life force" of the motorcycle vibrating through the hand rests. Then preside over this energy with a sense of delicate pressure. Never slam, jam, whack, crack, crank or yank on the controls. Use soft pressure instead. As you coax the controls, imagine three single silken threads delicately extending from your clutch, brake, and throttle, each disappearing into its appropriate housing on your motorcycle. Use light pressure on these threads. Infuse them with smoothness. Think smooth. Feel smooth all the while! As you think, so you become.

Good motorcycle form looks a little like that of a jockey on a racehorse, just not quite as extreme. Whenever you approach anything that requires more of your attention, sit more like a jockey. Lean forward and stay relaxed. You must be loose. Fake it, force it, do what you have to, but do it!

Set and reset this basic seating position often. Remember, the journey toward becoming a better rider is a journey of change. By simply improving your seating position as necessary, you've taken a major step on the journey—just like that!

Reading the Road
Part 1
Introduction to the Vanishing Point and the Scan

A rider intending to fuse with the road can no longer look through his helmet visor as if he is looking through a four-wheeler's windshield. Instead, a rider must learn to read the road. With practice, you will be a more confident and safer rider. You'll have a hell of a lot more fun, too.

I was first introduced to the concept of "reading the road" by another rider who was clearly farther along the never-ending journey toward getting better. He certainly rode his motorcycle better than I rode mine. It was nearly 20 years ago on a Sunday morning romp through the West Virginia countryside. I was with a small group of riding enthusiasts on one of my "Second Sunday Rides." These were events I organized monthly for regular and potential customers of the motorcycle dealership where I worked.

* * *

That Sunday, a new guy appeared. He stood out because, unlike the regulars geared in the latest attire, his look was "vintage." He wore a pair of black high-top sneakers, faded jeans, work gloves that had seen time in the dirt, and a weatherworn brown leather jacket. He was dressed more for a Sunday walk with the dog than for a sporting day of motorcycling. One hint that there was perhaps more to the new guy than he let on was the shiny, lightweight, and brightly-colored helmet he wore.

He rode an unusual motorcycle as well. It was a stubby, 25-year-old flat black BMW airhead. It was mostly stock with a few thoughtful upgrades. I noticed a top-of-the-line rear suspension, Italian carburetors, a chunky six gallon gas tank, low-set handlebars and hard-to-find Albert bar-end mirrors. Sweet! I clearly recall the motorcycle because the R75/5 had been my dream machine the year I entered college.

Over breakfast, we introduced ourselves. His name was Mike. He looked to be in his late 30s. His countenance was clean-shaven and boyish under a fresh buzz cut, making him seem younger than he was. His crinkly, direct, blue-eyed gaze, strong handshake and overall quietly confident manner left a favorable impression. During breakfast, as the chatter wound around the table, Mike kept to himself, with only a polite nod of agreement accompanied by an occasional faint smile.

Finally, with the bill paid and the proverbial tires kicked, we saddled up, and in a clamor of barking exhausts, sped off. The "ride-to-the-ride" rolled routine. Once we got into the good stuff, though, our group etiquette collapsed. As we were winding down a sweeping valley road, over my left shoulder, I heard the mechanical thrum of an accelerating /5 and—hello! I just got passed by Mike, the new guy!

Now don't get me wrong, I've been passed plenty— just not by some new guy in a group I was supposed to be leading, and certainly not by someone riding 25-year-old iron. Piqued, I downshifted, pinned the throttle on my faster steed and tried like mad to keep up.

Until that moment, I thought I was a good rider. And besides, my much newer mount had at least 20 horses on him. I just had to hang in! Barreling into a left curve, steep-leaning with the outside berm inches away, I spooked. If I hung in, I'd crash. Luckily better angels prevailed. I rolled off the throttle, released my death grip and, astonished, watched Mike steep-leaning pretty-as-you-please until—poof! He disappeared. As for me? My ass—sunny side up— had just been served!

The plan was for the group to reassemble several miles down the road at a distinctive rocky outcropping called Seneca Rocks State Park. I rode in, spiked on adrenaline and bug-eyed. Mike was already there, helmet off, casually fussing with his bike, a smoke dangling from his lips. His high-speed roll hadn't fazed him one whit. Grinning large, looking more boyish than ever, he was clearly and unselfconsciously having fun. I rolled into a space a few over from his and set my side-stand. Instead of swinging off the bike in a huff, I just sat there a moment feeling reflective as the engine heat ticked down. The more I thought, the more I felt: The heck with ego! I wanted to know how in the hell he served me up so easily. So I walked over and asked a few questions.

Unfortunately, Mike was not forthcoming. He was nice enough but didn't say much, other than that he was real pleased he read that stretch of road so well. "Read the road?" What was that? I had never considered "reading a road." I could hardly wait to get back to the dealership to ask Paul just how a motorcyclist "reads a road."

The following day, Paul shared his two-step strategy for reading a road: First acknowledge the vanishing point then scan the pavement. Simple. After seeing Mike fly, I bought into this strategy, made it my own, and have been practicing it ever since. Using this technique, my mind evaluates road detail most others simply don't see. It enables me to evaluate quickly, thoroughly, and effortlessly. I have confidence I otherwise would not have. I ride way more safely, and a wee bit faster, too.

* * *

The first step to reading a road is to find and acknowledge the vanishing point. Whenever you ride a road, notice that your line-of-sight always disappears at some point down the road. That point, where the road visually ends, is called the vanishing point. On a long, flat, straight road, the road vanishes from view at a point on the far horizon. Lines-of-sight also disappear around curves and over the crests of hills. For example, when a road curves to the left, notice that the landscape along the left converges with the roadway on the right. Where it converges and appears to end, be that near or far, is the vanishing point. The same thing occurs when a road curves right. The landscape along the right converges with the road on the left, and at some point, near or far, the road once again vanishes. That's the vanishing point. Approach the crest of any hill and you will notice the road will appear to vanish just at the crest of that hill. That too is the vanishing point.

Continuously anticipate and acknowledge the vanishing point. Practice this until you can't get it wrong. Developing this skill is non-negotiable and must always be uppermost in your spatial awareness. Why is this so important? The act of acknowledging the vanishing point places your attention on your immediate future: Where you are riding to next.

Being caught unaware or startled creates anxiety no matter what you are doing. This is certainly true when motorcycling. Untrained riders tend to keep their eyes roughly 20-40 feet ahead. When their eyes are fixed at such a short distance, they're going to descend upon potential problems with little to no warning and likely have zero time to respond to whatever issues might present themselves. Instead of maximizing safety and fun, they're going to wind up being exactly where they don't want to be: Caught with their pants down—anxious or startled. Continuously and deliberately lifting your eyes up and off the pavement in front of you and deliberately moving your attention farther down the road—to the vanishing point—gives you the most distance and the most time to evaluate critical details for that segment of road—the segment between where you are now and the vanishing point. That's important! Looking far afield relaxes you, which gives you better ability to see and respond to issues of safety. It also maximizes the fun factor by allowing you to more proactively respond to the pavement you will soon encounter.

The second part of this procedure is to sharpen your scan. The scan is your quick study of the road surface and general road environment between the vanishing point and you. But quick doesn't mean hasty. Don't rush! Be thorough. Train your eyes to calmly register any and every important detail on the road surface or along the sides of the road that could affect the safety and quality of your ride. Learning to scan effectively is non-negotiable. You must do this! Also, to make it easier on yourself—slow down!

Reading the Road Part 1

State-sponsored motorcycle safety courses at one time used the acronym S.I.P.D.E. meaning Scan (with your eyes), Identify (threats), Predict (what will happen), Decide (what to do), and Execute (your decision). They later boiled it down to S.E.E.: Search-Evaluate-Execute. If either acronym helps you to put these visual and cognitive skills into action, use it.

Rely on your peripheral vision for screening the shoulders of the road. Your peripheral vision doesn't focus well, but it is great at detecting movement. If your peripheral vision picks up any movement or any thing that grabs your attention—such as the flick of a whitetail— acknowledge it. Turn your eyes toward it, evaluate it, decide what to do, and then do it. Indecision can be costly. Afterwards, snap your eyes back to the vanishing point, and continue focusing on down the road.

Paul also pointed out something most people don't realize: Whenever your eyeballs are moving, you cannot see, period. That's right! You are essentially blind while your eyeballs are actually in motion. Prove it to yourself by looking in the mirror. Try to watch your eyeballs as they move from side to side. You can't do it. If you cannot see your eyes move, you can't see anything! It's important, therefore, as you ride, to move your eyes quickly and then pause your eyes long enough to focus and absorb pertinent detail—only then do you let them move on. Focus your eyes one or two more times along the expanse of pavement between you and the approaching vanishing point to accurately evaluate the traction or anything else you deem important. Then deliberately move those eyeballs to the next vanishing point and repeat the scanning process. You can then ride with the safe assumption that the road surface before you hasn't changed substantively between those brief eye movements. Then pause them again long enough to focus for another determination.

Try to capture the vanishing point quickly, but don't fret if your mind gets absorbed with assessing something important. Pay attention and practice. Practice moving your eyes to the vanishing point. Practice pausing your eyes. Practice focusing and absorbing. Purposely practice. The more practice you get, the better you will "slow" the environment down—in your mind. That's right! Think of big league batting champions. They take in tens of thousands of reps in a batting cage over a career. These batters are able to "slow" a fastball streaking toward them—in their mind—to the point that they are able to literally read the laces. You can do the same. Capture all the vanishing points, and then evaluate the road surfaces at various points along the pavement. With practice, you too will become a pro at reading the "laces" of the road environment.

As you practice, notice how you feel. Are you tense? Are you bored? Or are you focused and having fun? Ride slow enough to develop the skill but fast enough to keep things interesting. It's a balancing act. Keep moving your eyes. Never focus for too long on any one detail.

Be aware also that when you do encounter a hazard, your focus can unintentionally lock onto it. This is called "target fixation." If you encounter a hazard up ahead, have the calm presence of mind—gained from good posture and not riding too fast—to force your eyes away from that threat to where the road is clear, and steer a path toward it. Don't focus on the problem. Look toward the solution and go there.

There is an exception to moving your eyes to and from the vanishing point, and that's when the vanishing point is moving quickly. The only time a vanishing point moves is when you are leaning through a curve. The tighter the curve, the closer the vanishing point is to you, and the faster it moves. Curves can be so tight, with the vanishing point so close and moving so fast, that you don't have time to move your eyes off it. That's okay. Ride your own ride at a speed where you are comfortable processing the pavement details at the vanishing point as it moves in those tight curves. It's very doable given that the vanishing point is up close and that, again, you are not riding too fast.

Anytime you've crept outside posted speed limits, govern your speed by how you feel. Any time you feel tense, slow down! Leaning through a curve can generate sensory overload—as I had while chasing the "new guy." Tight curves are unnerving and can be dangerous to an inexperienced motorcyclist. I've had plenty of open-road "high milers" show up in my Workshops in their sun-faded riding gear and travel stickers adorning their saddlebags, and ride like rookies when they encounter their first several-mile stretch of successive Appalachian ridge line curves. Nowhere else in the country are there twisties like these. Ride them too fast, and your concentration and comprehension can jam. ("I just didn't see the gravel!") The time it takes to lean through a curve, chasing its vanishing point, can seem instantaneous. Nothing is still. The vanishing point flutters. Road details start passing under you like a blurry torrent of gushing water. These curves can easily choke an untrained mind. It's dizzying. Overwhelming. Now, OMG — it's happening to you!! Fear tunnels your vision. You stiff-arm! Red alert! Without Lady Luck—splat.

* * *

Practice riding more slowly as you strive to develop skill and confidence. Develop this two-step skill of seeking the vanishing point and scanning the pavement into a one-two punch of proficiency. When you do, you'll see more, your confidence will blossom, and soon you will naturally want to start rolling on more juice. Paradoxically, more speed is the natural result of first slowing down to see more—more clearly. With practice you'll soon ride like Mike, "the new guy!"

Reading the Road
Part 2
The Mantra

Confidence is essential if you ever hope to experience the thrill of the sport of sport-tour motorcycling. The increasing awareness that you are getting better, and feeling stronger for it, is its essence. But confidence isn't just handed out. It's earned by regular practice with an earnest intent to get better. The old saw goes: "Practice makes perfect." The more you practice, the better you get, the logical extension being: "The better you get, the more you like it! The more you like it, the more you do it. The more you do it, the better you get." So, regular practice, with a progressively successful outcome, is a Zen-like, closed-loop confidence generator!

However, just wanting to get better or wanting more confidence isn't enough. Simply wanting to get better keeps you stuck in a state of perpetual wanting. Changing wanting to intending shifts the mental focus toward a result! But only intending to get better or only intending to have more confidence still isn't enough. The key to getting the desired results is to intend to get better at something specific.

The specific skill that I'm going to share is taught at every racetrack and at every flight school across the country. I've taught this particular skill in my Workshop from Day One. The skill I am referring to is developing your "line." Your line is the mental structure for maximum safety that I mentioned earlier. I first learned the importance of lines in pilot training. Lines (compass headings) are utterly relevant when the view outside the cockpit window resembles the view from inside a ping-pong ball. Flying precise compass headings alone kept me safe. On a motorcycle, learning and "flying" precise lines is going to keep you safe too.

Learning the line is non-negotiable. You need to picture in your mind an optimally safe line over which you make your motorcycle pass, and then imagine your tires as a "paintbrush" to paint that line. Your tire track is the "line" that you "paint." Your task is to mentally envision your safest line and then deliberately paint it.

At the racetrack, the goal of the so-called "perfect line" is speed. On public roads—and especially mountain roads—the purpose of the line is safety. Develop great lines, especially through curves, and you will automatically become a safer, better rider no matter what or where you ride.

***

The Beautiful Paradox

You will become proficient too with all of its benefits! One benefit of proficiency is speed. That's right! Being proficient at something means you're going to be naturally faster at getting that "something" done. As it pertains to motorcycling, I call it the "Beautiful Paradox." The Beautiful Paradox of sport-touring is that while riders immerse themselves in the Zen-like pursuit of the safest line, they tend to naturally ride faster and lean steeper and have a lot more FUN in the process. I repeat: Speed is the natural result of improved proficiency! Speed is not the objective, it's the byproduct. These riders ride faster and have more FUN, all the while riding as safely as a motorcyclist possibly can. That's why I call it the "Beautiful Paradox"!

* * *

Remember that to become better, you must change, and change isn't easy. I have captured the structure for painting the safest line in the form of a mantra, not in a short acronym. Take whatever time you need to memorize it. It's the blueprint for visualizing your line. The mantra creates the mental structure within which you ride. By memorizing the mantra to the extent you truly internalize it, you will have changed. When you do, good things will happen. Here it is:

ANTICIPATE CONTINUOUSLY. NOW PRECISELY PRE-POSITION MYSELF FIRST FOR SAFETY, THEN FOR TRACTION AND THEN FOR THE ABSOLUTE CLEAREST VIEW OF THE VANISHING POINT.

By surrendering your ego and committing this mantra to memory, and then by *demonstrating* the skills behind these words, you will begin to transform into an uncommonly skillful motorcyclist. To aid in memorization, the key words of the mantra are alphabetical as well as hierarchical. Let's study them one word at a time before you take the mantra out on the road.

ANTICIPATE CONTINUOUSLY. "A" before "C." This means, always be thinking ahead. Expert riders are continuously thinking ahead. Their minds aren't distracted. They are continuously focused on what's coming next.

There are two dominant aspects of a ride to anticipate: Safety and fun. When issues of safety arise, anticipate your "out." Ride at such a speed that, on the fly, you can always develop a safer alternative line should your chosen line deteriorate. Anticipating the movement of traffic relative to you is especially important. Many accidents could have been avoided if the motorcyclist had anticipated that the vehicle was going to abruptly turn left in front of them.

As for the element of fun, fun will always depend on the conditions you're riding through. But the more you develop a sense of oneness with your motorcycle, and the better you become at reading the road, the more fun you will have on any road you choose. By using your own creativity and applying your motorcycle's special performance characteristics to a particular stretch of road, you create conditions for pure enjoyment as you ride.

NOW! It means just that. Do what you need to do—this instant! Do it at once! Be sharp. Be crisp. Be firm. Be smooth. And do it now! Don't let your mind wander, especially on mountain roads.

PRECISELY PRE-POSITION. This means two things: The first is positioning your motorcycle on the pavement exactly where you want it to be for the next instant of travel. The second meaning is a little trickier: You need to be at the exact speed you want to be for the next instant of pavement. For example, precisely pre-positioned speed means being at a certain speed just as you arrive at a curve's entrance point, so in the next instant you can accelerate as you enter the curve. In summary, pre-positioning means precise placement as well as precise speed for the next instant of the ride.

FIRST FOR SAFETY. There are no exceptions to safety! Safety first. Safety last. Safety forever more. However, with experience, a rider's perception of safety evolves. Riders who have attended my Workshop have already learned to unconditionally accept that absolute safety comes first. It's implicit! They are now interested in ascending beyond pure safety to the nuanced mental, physical, emotional, technical, and Zen-like realms of expert motorcycling. I therefore summarize far-reaching safety (knowing there are plenty of other books on the subject of safety) like this: Don't hit anything; don't get hit; and don't fall off. This may seem trite, but I mean every word.

THEN FOR TRACTION. Once a rider understands the ironclad requirement for continuous safety, the subtler need for continuous traction can be addressed. Make sure your line is continuously on a surface with adequate traction. The pavement is a continuous study. This is true, of course, no matter where you ride, but it is especially so in the mountains where you're going to face questionable traction—in ever-changing ways. It's often around the next curve and/or when it's least expected.

Traction in sodden conditions is every motorcyclist's concern. There are plenty of riders who are spooked by rain and, when given the choice, simply won't ride in it. It's difficult to measure traction just by looking at it. In general, stay on dull-looking pavement and keep off slick-looking pavement. But all the staring in the world won't give you as much knowledge as a few moments spent feeling the pavement.

So, personally, that's what I do—I feel it. That's right! I take my waterproof boot off the foot peg and lightly skim the sole across the pavement. I learn much more about my immediate traction by feeling the pavement than by simply looking at it. Often, I am pleasantly surprised. If the pavement is at all grippy, I know my modern motorcycle tires will have plenty of traction for the appropriately modest speeds I intend to use. Other times, I am rather stunned to find that while the pavement looks okay, the road is so slick and the quality of traction so nearly non-existent that I need to slow WAY down—right now! This is often true in areas of congested traffic where petroleum waste has accumulated on the pavement. It's also true on tar-and-chipped country roads where much of the "chip" has worn away leaving mostly just the slippery "tar."

Once I was riding through an area that ten minutes earlier had obviously had a hard rain because the pavement and surroundings were soaking wet. I approached a clearly-marked 15 MPH 90-degree right-hand curve, one that I had ridden thru many times before, and thought I had adequately slowed down so as to be able to lightly accelerate up a small rise just beyond the turn. In an instant, I was slammed to the pavement. "What the...??" Luckily, I wasn't hurt. Stunned, yes. Dinged, yes. The bike had to be towed. I walked the several yards back to the small rise and discovered a large tar patch, slicker than slick, as if it had been oiled. My front tire had washed out, and BOOM! I was down. Stuff happens that fast.

It's hard to imagine a rider who is not wary of poor traction on gravel/oil/sand/mud/tar/icy/wet pavement and crashing. But you have got to see it! And yet, several years ago I was riding with a group of fellas who were all good riders. From their expensive gear and late-model sport-tourers, I knew they took their motorcycling seriously. At one point, I was riding behind one of those riders who was riding well.

His line was deliberate and he rode smoothly. Along one ten-mile stretch of beautifully clean pavement, he upped his pace into a nice groove. Then, suddenly, around a routine middle-gear right-hander, he plowed right into a two-foot wide, thirty-foot long, quarter-inch thick expanse of fine gravel. In a heartbeat, his wheels lost grip, his rear wheel swung wide, then abruptly re-caught traction, and he launched! Regrettably he damaged both his beautiful red motorcycle and himself. As for the rest of us, his lack of attention wrecked our afternoon, too. And it didn't have to happen.

To ride safely, you must preserve traction at all times. Otherwise, the consequences will likely be unpleasant.

CLEAREST VIEW OF THE VANISHING POINT. Once the two priority issues of safety and traction are fully addressed, the final concept in the mantra is to precisely place your motorcycle on the road surface for the clearest view of the vanishing point. The vanishing point is where the road disappears from view. Think of the vanishing point as a bullseye. The objective is to position your motorcycle continuously on the pavement so your eyes can rest clearly on that bullseye—just like a marksman does with a gunsight. With this concept of a bullseye in mind, think of a road in terms of segments: The length of each segment extends from where you are now to the vanishing point ahead. By continuously placing your motorcycle for the clearest view of the next vanishing point, you again give yourself the most time and the most distance to deal with whatever is critical to your safety, or adds to your fun, within that segment of roadway. Aim your bike from bullseye to bullseye. Stitch as many of these segments together as precisely as you can.

The vanishing point is most dynamic when you ride curvy roads. It will dance to the left, then juke to the right, move up close, then move far away. It'll speed up. It'll slow down. The curvier the road, the more rapidly it moves; the tighter the curve, the faster it moves until it matches your own speed.

To maintain the clearest view of the vanishing point on curvy roads, a rider must continuously study it and react in order to pass through that clearest path on the road. The tighter the curve, the closer the vanishing point is to you, the faster the vanishing point moves and the faster a rider must think and react to stay positioned.

The mental strength realized by reciting the mantra from your saddle while out on the road is more powerful than simply memorizing it from the cushion of your comfy chair. You will have a comprehensive skill set to polish 100 percent of the time your wheels are rolling. That this statement is powerful is an understatement! Reciting the mantra out on the trail will forge you into the safe and accomplished motorcyclist you intend to become. Each word's meaning will percolate into your awareness and prompt you to paint something safe, something meaningful, something enjoyable and FUN every moment of your ride.

Riders who paint a "mantra-driven" line are safer and have more fun. Committing the mantra to memory is the giant leap in your progress from the ordinary motorcyclist you might be today into the exceptional motorcyclist you intend to become. It is this continued practice with an earnest intent to get better that separates expert riders from average ones. Memorizing and repeating the mantra places you on and keeps you on the journey toward mastery. It's that simple.

Reading the Road
Part 3
The Line: A Mental Structure for Safety

During any typical ride, the reality is that a tiny percentage of time is spent dealing with critical issues of safety and/or traction. A far greater percentage of the time is spent pre-positioning yourself for the clearest view of the vanishing point. By having a marksman's bullseye view of the target, you give yourself more distance and time. This in turn creates space for more safety and fun. The following is the mental structure I use for continuously employing the mantra for lane positioning. It's my nitty-gritty for getting the job done. It should work for you, too. So here we go!

Take any two-lane road. It might have a painted centerline, or maybe it's a half-lane road with no markings. Visualize your side of the road as being divided into three longitudinal mini-lanes—like bowling lanes. Your left mini-lane is located just to the right of the center of the entire road. Your middle mini-lane is located in the center of your side of the road. And finally, your right mini-lane is located far to the right, parallel to the road's right shoulder, along a white fog line if there is one.

We all enjoy motorcycling on hills and curves, but reality dictates that roads often run flat and straight. The vanishing point on a flat road remains visible and motionless in the distance. Whenever a road runs mostly straight, theoretically, the best view of the vanishing point is from the very middle of the road - right on the centerline imaginary or painted. Therefore, on flat, straight roads with a centerline, position your motorcycle in the left mini-lane on your side of the road. If the road has no actual centerline, position your motorcycle in the center of the road. Theoretically, this gives you the best view of the road ahead.

On straight roads, consider the left mini-lane as being your default riding position where you regularly return. It's your "home" lane. There are four reasons for doing this: First, you will have the clearest view of the vanishing point. Second, you assert yourself onto oncoming traffic for better conspicuity and safety. Third, you place yourself equidistant from "wildcard" threats possibly bolting from the sides of the roadway, the most dangerous and quite common being whitetail deer. And, fourth, you give yourself something active to do: Intentionally keeping your motorcycle precisely positioned. This keeps you riding attentively "in the moment." Riders who are riding attentively in the moment are safer than riders who aren't. Believe it!

Let's assume now you that you're motoring along in your "home position" in the left mini-lane. You have the clearest view of the vanishing point. When oncoming traffic presents itself, make a small but de-deliberate shift to the left side of your left mini-lane. That's right! Snug against the centerline. This is visually disturbing to any normal oncoming driver— one who's paying attention, that is! From the oncoming driver's perspective, you appeared to be riding right down the center of the road and now you've made a small move just a tad more to the left! "What is he doing??" they wonder. Alert drivers will typically respond by moving well to the right side of their lane away from center. If they don't, YOU might need to then be concerned: Either they are not paying attention, or they are not functioning normally. Maybe they are drunk, doped, or simply distracted. Or maybe he or she is an aggressive driver with something to prove! If so, just give a friendly wave as you ride by. The point is, you have asserted yourself. You are now inescapably being seen and being acknowledged by oncoming traffic.

Does this mean that you "play chicken" and just remain in the middle of the road as the approaching traffic gets closer? Of course not! You assert your presence and then simply move your motorcycle into your middle or rightmost mini-lane before the vehicle passes. Afterward, resume your default position in the left mini-lane. This kind of positioning results in sort of a radar "ping" off that oncoming traffic, and you are getting a "reading" back from it.

The Art of Riding Smooth

"Are you awake?" "Are you sober?" "Are you paying attention?" Is this pro-active defensive motorcycling? Absolutely!

Have you ever been concerned that you are not being seen by oncoming traffic, especially if a vehicle looks as though it's about to turn in front of you? If so, slightly swerve and perhaps flash your high beam, and certainly cover your brakes. This is also pro-active defensive motorcycling. I call this safety mindset being "defensively offensive." Around traffic, I am rarely reactive. Why? Anticipation! Mentally I'm usually a step ahead of traffic. Traffic can't help but see me, and that is the point, isn't it? Using aviation parlance, the mindset is to be continuously "pilot in command" of the situation—any situation—and especially around other traffic.

Riding in your left mini-lane on rural and suburban roads affords you better separation from anything that might dash from either side of the road: Critters, people rushing to check their mailbox, vehicles abruptly entering the road, and especially deer.

Deer hooves on pavement are a little like leather-soled shoes on ice—very poor traction. Deer dash from the woods, hit the pavement, then scramble, slip, slide, and sometimes fall. This frantic effort to gain traction on their part gives you fractions of a second to stop, swerve or squeak by.

Deer, like dogs, are crepuscular, meaning they are on the move at dawn and dusk. I've seen plenty of browsing deer during these hours and especially at night. Even with extra caution, I've had a few close calls. On one ride alone, twice I saw deer slip and stumble on the pavement just ahead of me. On a different ride, I saw the tiniest fawn frantically barrel-roll trying to make its escape! It did. During those tense moments, I slowed and snugged the centerline, thus surrounding myself with maximum pavement for wider avenues of avoidance left or right. Riding the centerline just might minimize the odds of an unwanted furry encounter, or something worse—as I witnessed several years ago.

It was early June and I was riding south, following a friend on the Blue Ridge Parkway headed for the great roads farther south. We both had new sets of tires; our bikes were freshly tuned. We were about 20 miles south of the Peaks of Otter Lodge. He was ahead of me as we came around a shallow left curve. There, on the right shoulder, was a small whitetail deer. Immediately, I could tell we had startled the deer by the way it jerked its head and stiffened its body. I snapped to the left mini-lane. My buddy did not. He was positioned in our right mini-lane closest to the deer and didn't budge. The deer bolted at the worst moment and smashed into my friend, slamming his motorcycle violently sideways and catapulting him into the air. Luckily, his trajectory was shallow as he went sailing into tall, wet grass. When he quit sliding, he stood up dazed and confused, a 20 foot debris-field trailing behind him, but with nary a scratch, thanks to good gear and all that slippery wet grass! The deer wasn't so lucky; neither was his bike. Both were totaled. My thinking was that had he hugged the centerline, there may have been an instant for him to slip by and avoid the collision, but of course, we'll never know. Since a deer bolting out of nowhere is the great "wildcard" in motorcycling, I say keep yourself and your motorcycle surrounded by as much pavement as you can. It's similar to the pilot's proverb: "You can never have too much fuel aboard, too much runway ahead of you, or too much altitude below you."

When I was flying my airplane, there were long periods of tedious straight and level flight. To take the boredom out of those phases of flight, I made a point of flying with pinpoint accuracy. I'd take the airplane off auto-pilot and hand-hold my course line to within a tenth of a mile from my GPS-generated centerline. If the skies were clear, I'd watch the ground to determine exactly where I was. I did this by matching details on the ground with details on my flight chart. By demanding precision from myself, I could sense course deviations and make corrections before I wandered off course. The added benefit was that this gave my mind something engaging to do. Working on my precision kept me occupied and alert as I cruised up high during those long straight-and-level hours.

Whenever I am motorcycling on relatively long, flat or straight roads, I try to demand that same precision. My position is always intentionally in the left mini-lane until, for a good reason, I decide to be somewhere else on the pavement. This vigilance keeps me active and alert where most others allow themselves to absentmindedly drone along.

Positioning in curves is different. Entering and riding through a curve is where anticipation and precision should be forefront in your mind. Curves are also where the fun begins! As a general rule, left-hand curves are trickier than right-hand curves and a little nerve-wracking to ride precisely. When approaching left-hand curves, pre-position your motorcycle in your right mini-lane. Positioning yourself on the right of the lane gives you the best right-to-left line-of-sight to the vanishing point through the curve. However, entering and leaning into a left curve from the right mini-lane can sometimes cause you to feel anxious, as if you're going to go wide and off the right edge of the road. If you ever feel like this, anticipate this feeling for the next left-hand curve and prepare. The key is to slow down. It's just so critically important to ride at a speed at which you can comfortably assess the important visual cues in the curve environment between you and the vanishing point so that you can then comfortably carve a precise line for safety and fun. Safety is sometimes an issue. Fun is nearly always the issue. Getting proficient at precise curve-carving is FUN!

As you reach the entry point of a left curve (where you and your motorcycle would begin to lean) be patient. Don't rush to initiate the left counter-steer and lean in. Wait—until you see the vanishing point just begin to move away—before you lean the bike over into the left-hand lean. A pinch of patience with precise steering inputs will keep your bike tracking in the right mini-lane (or at least the right side of the middle mini-lane) as you lean into the curve. This ensures safe clearance from both the centerline and right borderline throughout the entire curve.

If or when you do feel tension, deliberately move your eyes toward the center of the roadway or over to the left-hand side of the roadway and steer your motorcycle toward that. You might also apply a bit of rear brake. This will cause the bike to lean in a little easier. On the other hand, if you somehow find yourself riding too close to the centerline too early, place your eyes on the right berm or white fog line or even accelerate a bit to widen your line. This effort will "pull" you back toward the right, where you know you belong.

If you botch a curve, don't fret. Let the tension go. Don't carry tension from one curve to the next. Tension is cumulative. Take a deep breath, release the tension, and get ready for the next curve and the next. There are plenty more curves to come.

Approach right-hand curves from the left mini-lane for the best left-to-right sight line. As you approach the entry point for a right-hand curve, move your motorcycle away from the left mini-lane into the middle or right mini-lane. Again, this allows you separation from the centerline with an adequate left-to-right line-of sight to clearly watch the vanishing point and other road details. If the right mini-lane is clear, clean of debris and nicely banked, I often take the shortest "racing line" by tucking deep to the right around those tight right-hand curves. I can better steep lean, and if it's an "S" curve, I'll exit the right-hander positioned nicely for the immediately upcoming left-hander.

Riders with little training often approach curves from anywhere they happen to be on the pavement. Through left curves, they lean in too early and bust the centerline. Through right curves, they'll lean too late, bust the centerline and go wide. This is sloppy motorcycling and a recipe for a "close encounter of the metallic kind."

Just recently, I was on a beautiful autumn ride down the Blue Ridge Parkway with a group of seasoned motorcyclists. The lead rider and I were chatting via Bluetooth devices. At one point, he busted the double yellow around a right-hand curve. The instructor in me couldn't help but point out his error, and he responded, "Sorry.. DAD." So I kept my mouth shut. At another point not much later, I had the lead. This same rider was now third in line. As we rolled along, I commented that, at the pace we were rolling, deliberate precision was essential. He actually agreed, but talk is cheap. Then, not fifteen seconds later, I heard a crash through my helmet speakers! I'll be damned if he didn't go wide again—and again through a right-hand curve. Only this time, he glanced off an SUV! Luckily he didn't hit the vehicle head on. If he had, he likely would have been killed. Instead, he smashed the driver's side window and tore off the sideview mirror. He hit the vehicle so hard that he broke out the rear window and later learned that he had totaled the SUV! This rider knew better, and I had just forewarned him! And he was no rookie, either. In fact, he had prided himself on all the hundreds of thousands of miles he'd ridden. Luckily, he only got banged up. Afterward, he sheepishly told me he was going to sign up for a Workshop the following season.

Over the years, I have seen many riders dodge close calls, known several riders who have been seriously injured, and know of a few fatal accidents caused by riders colliding with vehicles too near the centerline or pulling in front of them. Continuous anticipation and precision are again the two primary keys to safety no matter when or where you ride.

One can never tell what's happening on the backside of hill crests. Hedge your bet by cresting hills in the middle mini-lane. Further hedge your bet by having great posture, being on your toes (literally) just as you crest the hilltop, then grab the next vanishing point! By being centered in the middle mini-lane and being alert, you will best be able to quickly assess the curve's backside and make any necessary safety adjustment.

Here's a tip: Southeast Ohio, around the greater Marietta Area, boasts wide-ranging roads that are as challenging as any in the United States. Lack of glacial activity thousands of years ago and continuous water erosion gouged the land into narrow ravines and winding valleys with many switching back on themselves. The roads are twistier than most riders have ever experienced. What's more, the twists are hidden. Rollercoaster-like blind crests in quick succession conceal the twists, coils and corkscrews, and variations in pavement quality on the backside view. It's on extremely technical roads like these that keen attention to your line and posture will help keep you safe, as well as amp up the fun.

It's important to acknowledge that stationary or slow-moving roadway hazards rarely present themselves immediately. It's not as if these threats magically or instantly pop into full view. Obvious hazards present themselves progressively. This is particularly true around blind curves and over blind crests. For example, an entire farm tractor doesn't just appear on the far side of a blind crest. In reality, you'll first see the uppermost structure of the tractor, perhaps its exhaust stack, and as you get closer, the rest of the tractor's features will progressively appear. I cannot over-emphasize the need to ride at a speed where you can comfortably evaluate the road environment for such hazards. Carefully read the road, and then take simple evasive action whenever necessary. The mindset for riding unfamiliar technical roads is to expect the unexpected. This is especially true for indistinct hazards like poor traction. You often don't see the cause for poor traction until you're almost on top of it. That's why it's best to be ready—expecting that exhaust stack, lousy traction, or anything else unnerving in areas of short visibility.

But stuff happens. Unexpected hazards can scare the hell out of you, or worse. As an example of a hazard showing up unexpectedly, once I was riding just west of Monterey, Virginia on Route 250, headed for the Blue Grass Valley. I was on my game too, expecting the unexpected, when my tires rolled over a wide swirl of gravel spread dangerously across a tight curve. The situation absorbed nearly all of my mental bandwidth. I had to simultaneously reconfigure a brand new line and ride it in tight, in downhill conditions. Then, suddenly on the backside of this corkscrew, the bug-splattered grill of a hard-working Peterbilt appeared chugging up the other side — hogging my lane! I clearly remember what happened next: My focus doubled down, and I calmly aimed the motorcycle for the far right side of the right mini-lane, as I had often planned to do in such a circumstance. That is the safest place when confronted with a vehicle hogging your rightful space on a road. That's where I knew to go, that's where I pre-planned to go, and that's where I went! And, I am happy to report, that's how I was able to squeak around that massive semi-truck.

Your line is different on narrow roads with no centerline. When on straightaways, position your motorcycle in the middle of the entire road for the best view of the vanishing point. However, around both left and right curves, position your bike strategically in the right mini-lane. This defensive positioning usually gives you separation from oncoming traffic around both left and right curves—but not always! It's only a matter of time before a local vehicle will come barreling along, driven by some testosterone-addled adolescent male, swerving into your path while reaching for that smartphone on the floor! Around those tighter curves, edge over to the right edge of your right mini-lane, mindful that you don't stumble off the pavement or get caught in a rut. Ride tight right, but look left!

I remember once riding alone along a favorite "invisible road" (more on this term later) outside Franklin, West Virginia. I was motoring up a fairly steep grade topped with a blind crest. I tucked in tight to the right, practicing what I preach, when without warning, a dairy truck came flying out of the vanishing point! If I had not been tucked in tight to the far right, I don't think I would be alive today. Another three feet to the left and I would have been creamed (pun intended) into the grill of that big rig. Here's a review from one of my Workshop riders who makes the same point:

"A few weeks ago, I took Jim's Workshop. I was hoping to become a more proficient rider, especially on twisty roads. The weather and the scenery were beautiful, and my fellow 'classmates' were friendly and encouraging. I certainly got what I came for.

"As a bonus, I learned a lot about true safety. I have always considered myself a cautious rider. I wear hi-viz clothing and I am conscious of the theory of 'conspicuity.' But Jim also taught me an important lesson about ensuring safety on country roads with blind crests and blind turns. Precise lines are important! At some point on the second day, Jim noticed my position on the road, and through his radio communication, admonished me in no uncertain terms that my position would be disastrous if a vehicle were coming the other way. On that particular rural road, with no real shoulders and no center or fog lines, even a car in its own lane would have hit me head-on. With that lesson still ringing in my ears, I kept much farther to the right, and less than a mile later, with me in the lead, a big green pick-up came around a blind corner. Talk about a timely tip!

"Jim said: If you want to ride the mountain roads safely, sharpen your mountain line; otherwise don't ride them!

"If you are serious about becoming a better, smoother, safer motorcyclist, drop him a line and sign up for his course." (Paul B., Oak Park, Illinois.)

Hopefully the concept of riding the mini-lanes will serve as the structure you use to help you climb to the loftier plateaus of motorcycling expertise, and fun. Riders who are riding intentionally within the mantra's structure are simply better, more confident, safer and faster riders simultaneously—guaranteed!

It's All About Curves

There are as many reasons to ride a motorcycle as there are people who ride them. As you have likely guessed, I'm a curve junkie. If my motorcycle isn't leaning into a curve, I don't feel like I'm really riding—but that's me. Others surely feel differently and that's fine. I lean toward the *sport* of sport-touring. Sporting through curves are the exclamation points that punctuate a great ride! You feel me? It's why I ride mountains since mountain curves are far and away the most exciting curves to ride.

My fascination with mountain curves reaches back to those early days sweating it out in the cockpit learning to fly an airplane. Flying an airplane and carving a curve both have a lot of moving pieces. Living in two dimensions is our earthbound human reality. In the air, enter the third dimension where it's altogether different—an acquired taste, I would say. Routine maneuvers in the third dimension, like simply turning around and flying in the opposite direction, require concentration and a lot of practice. The goal is to achieve a "standard rate" turn which is considered safe no matter what the atmospheric conditions are. A "standard rate" turn is a 180-degree turn in exactly one minute while maintaining a constant altitude. To accomplish this, a pilot must bank the airplane at 3 degrees of inclination for 60 seconds and hold altitude. This results in a 180-degree turn in one minute. To execute the turn, a pilot looks out the windows to check for traffic, banks the airplane to 3 degrees of incline, punches a stopwatch, pushes the throttle forward just so to hold airspeed, trims the elevators to hold altitude, concentrates on holding that 3 degrees of angle while keeping the plane's nose on the horizon line, and finally rolls out straight and level after exactly one minute.

Rolling out after one minute, the flight instruments either report a 180-degree turn with no change in altitude, or not. But I progressively got better and was eventually able to nail the maneuver every time; even 360s—just double the time. Aviating demands continuous attention, perfect practice and much repetition to gain the required proficiency. I loved the challenge!

Carving mountain curves on a motorcycle is much like banking an airplane. The maneuver requires continuous concentration, precision, and plenty of practice. It's rather three-dimensional, too, since curves often ascend or descend, and the forward view banks as well.

My fascination with curves is the reason why I ride almost exclusively in the Appalachian Mountains. This is the largest region of concentrated curves found anywhere in the United States!

IT'S ALL ABOUT CURVES

Before I get into an explanation of carving curves, allow me to briefly describe why I love these mountains. If you love riding curves, you'll fall like mad for them too!

First of all, the Appalachians were once similar in size to the more glamorous Alps, Andes, Himalayas, and Rockies, but that was eons ago. The Appalachians are now more like worn molars - crumbled by decay. Some geologists say they are the oldest mountains on the planet. Over millions of millennia, water and wind erosion have carved them into a complex patchwork of rolling hills, rocky ridgelines, meandering river valleys, deep forests, high meadows, steep ravines, and shaded hollows. In "them thar hills" there's still wilderness to be found!

The Appalachians once teemed with animal life that has since moved on, moved out, or become extinct. What's left is a vast landscape criss-crossed with former game trails that were once the primordial means of travel for forest beasts from one region to another. These trails often run along streams coursing downhill to the next larger body of water, continuing on until the streams form rivers such as (North to South) the Catoctin, Cacapon, Cheat, Dry Fork, Potomac, Jackson, James, Roanoke, Smith, Little, New, Holston, Clinch, French Broad and the Tennessee. I've ridden alongside them all.

Over the centuries, the best of these game trails were first trampled into footpaths and river walks by the Native People, then later by early settlers.

These footpaths were then worn further by ox cart and wagon trains into rutted, rocky roads until finally, these rocky roads were graded, graveled or paved-over for automobiles and, as luck would have it—our motorcycles!

I call these former game trails "invisible roads." An invisible road is just a local road, but unless you know the local road is there, it is "invisible" because it is typically not the most direct route between major population centers and thus, out of one's awareness. The AAA, for example, would never route you on these roads. Invisible roads are "out of mind." As such, intrepid riders who seek these invisible roads wind up there mostly alone, since thru-traffic is totally unaware these roads exist, and local traffic doesn't stay on local roads for very long. If only the locals know the roads are there, chances are you are going to have them all to yourself. You will be able to ride alone for miles and miles unimpeded by traffic! And isn't that a touch of ecstasy for us motorcyclists?

To ride these invisible roads well, you must understand the common characteristics of mountain curves and develop appreciation and respect for their details. Each curve is a separate entity. If you are attentive and respectful, you will be rewarded with thrills not found elsewhere. If you aren't, it's only a matter of time before you'll crash.

A curve can be broken down into four segments: The Approach, The Entry, The Curve Itself, and The Exit.

Each of these segments must be addressed individually.

The Approach

If you intend to carve a curve with any gusto, your preparation begins well before the curve itself. The sporting curves I am referring to are typically done in 1st, 2nd, 3rd, and perhaps 4th gear. Curves ridden in 5th and 6th gear are better termed "sweepers." Sweepers are more like straight roads with a bend in them—their vanishing points remain relatively still, so they don't count. Therefore, for this discussion, I am not addressing them.

As you approach a tighter curve, focus your attention on the curve's vanishing point. That's where you start. Rest your eyes on the vanishing point long enough to evaluate all of its unique details. Maybe you see a lot, maybe you see a little, but get into the habit of acknowledging the curve starting at its vanishing point, and get its measure as soon as its vanishing point presents itself.

The operative word is "anticipation." Anticipating well ahead gives you maximum distance and time to study a curve's unique characteristics. With this advanced knowledge and with experience, you will begin to accurately determine your best approach and proper entry speed, as well as being best prepared for what is just beyond your field of view.

The Art of Riding Smooth

Determining a safe entry speed during this approach phase is essential and cannot be over-emphasized. Mastering this is another non-negotiable skill and ranks near the top of all motorcycling skills!

Start by making an overall study of the basic visual cues surrounding every vanishing point. For example, if you are following a body of water, a stream, creek, or river, you can often expect a series of S-curves in many shapes and sizes, one curve flowing into the next. Not so with a railroad track. Roads paralleling railroad tracks or other engineered entities tend to run fairly straight. If there is a steep slope curtaining the back side of a curve, the curve is likely to follow the base of that slope and is likely to be asymmetrical and tight. If a guardrail or a tree line along the far shoulder of a curve is perpendicular to your approach, chances are again that the curve is likely to be tight.

Anticipate road camber or the slightly convex cross-road slope before entering the curve, since camber is not always obvious. If the right guardrail on a left curve seems lower than the roadbed or if your lane disappears over the crown of the road revealing only the oncoming lane, your lane into the curve is going to be off-camber and tilted away from the direction of the curve. Have you ever leaned into what looked like a perfectly good curve only to feel "on edge" as you leaned through? Revisit that curve and I'll bet it was off-camber. Off-camber curves are deceptive that way. Off-camber curves provide less traction and less clearance since you will be leaning in the opposite direction on a pavement that is tilting away from you. If that's the case, be prepared to feel less traction and perhaps scraping a toe or a foot peg, which is another reason to keep the balls of your feet tucked back on the foot peg. If this is the case, slow down! Off-camber curves aren't always obvious and a major factor why there are so many single rider crashes around curves. If there is gravel around an off-camber curve, you had better be ready, because you'll likely need to take evasive action to avoid it. Take it easy! Conversely, if a guardrail around that same left curve sits in plain view or is banked up slightly, the pavement is on-camber or banked toward the direction of the curve, giving you improved traction and clearance. On a positive-camber road your motorcycle will bank left without you even leaning it left since the pavement is already banking left. Less lean will be required, and thus traction is greatly improved. Got it? As for me, I'm crazy for on-camber. It's a priority. I seek it out. I like putting my suspension right across the most on-camber section of a curve. I'll then blip my throttle, compress the suspension, then "springboard" off the curve. YaHOO!

Around right-hand curves with wide shoulders, watch for gravel or strewn stones. Vehicles with trailers are often pulled through these stony shoulders, throwing all manner of detritus onto the pavement. Don't panic. If the quantity of stones is such that they can possibly be counted, they are considered strewn stones. Strewn stones are not like dense gravel and thus not as likely to upset your traction so completely that your tires lose traction and slide out from underneath you. If your tires bump, skid or otherwise protest while you are leaning through such a curve—hang in. At least you weren't spooked, and you'll be through the patch in a jiffy.

Gravel, though, is a thicker layer of uncountable stones and debris often pulverized to a fine sand. If the patch you encounter is thick enough that you cannot see pavement through it, and it is wide enough and long enough and you accelerate, lean, or otherwise plow into it unawares, then it's "Adios!" There is an excellent chance that both of your tires will lose all traction, and in an instant, you'll crash. A crash like this is nearly always your fault. The gravel didn't cause you to crash. You caused your crash because you failed to be attentive and respectful, and in command of your speed and lean angle. If you fail to see a hazard, you were likely riding too fast, or your mind was elsewhere!

Several years ago, I was riding with a group of mostly enduro riders along Potomac River bottomland. The roadway was a lane-and-a-half and mostly trended clear, although there were lots of mud puddles along our right shoulder. I was leading. Approaching one right-hander, I noticed the pavement turned very dark just as it disappeared into the curve. I dabbed the rear brake and, since the land was low and flat where I could see possible oncoming traffic, I went slightly wide, giving this dark area a wide berth. The rider two bikes behind me didn't. Instead, he willy-nilly plowed into what turned out to be mud! In a flash, his bike disappeared out from beneath him as both he and his machine went sliding—right into the longest, muddiest puddle you've ever seen. Was he a sight!! To top it off, he was wearing a fresh-out-of-the-box-that-morning all-weather leather riding suit. I guess he stayed dry, but his suit was a mess. And he stank! Luckily he wasn't hurt, his bike wasn't damaged and, being a good sport, he even managed a good laugh. But you must anticipate continuously!

Utility poles and electric wires surrounding a curve often "telegraph" which way a road is headed just beyond your view. If any wires are moving in a specific direction, the road will often curve in the same direction. Be prepared by evaluating a curve's surroundings. Don't get caught coming "hot" into a curve without any idea of what you're about to encounter at or just beyond the vanishing point.

A useful skill for those riding with a GPS device is to zoom in its range function to a couple tenths of a mile to magnify your immediate riding area. You can then glance at your GPS screen to preview the quality of the upcoming curves. While you can't see pavement details, you can determine if the curve is open or tight to get an idea of the speed you might need to shed before approaching the curve.

Judging your approach speed to a mountain curve is all-important. All of your slowing should be done during the approach analysis phase before you actually enter a curve; otherwise you will make problems for yourself.

It's best to arrive at your desired entry speed through executing a series of downshifts. When done smoothly, your suspension stays in its "sweet spot" for best grip, and you'll have just the right amount of torque. The moment you use your front brake, you shift weight, and the momentum moves off your rear suspension onto your front suspension. This transfer loosens your rear tire patch, making your bike feel less planted. If you need to use brakes, try gently pressing your rear brake, since that brake barely unsettles your suspension. Use your rear brake to finesse speed. Reserve using your front brake to authoritatively slow you down, or to come to a complete stop—which is not something you want to do when entering a mountain curve.

Pay attention to downshifting. Downshifting smoothly is a craft. Make every downshift count for smoothness. That's the goal - seamless smoothness. It's the obtainable high bar of gear shifting, and it's satisfying to practice. Smoothness makes for an easier transition to leaning the motorcycle once you've entered the curve. Strive for seamlessly smooth shifts. Practice shifting until you own this skill. Developing this skill is compulsory if you intend to develop expert ridership.

The most challenging curves are taken in the three lowest gears. Your goal is to work toward primarily using these gears, rather than the brakes, to slow down. The downshift from third gear into second gear is probably the most important downshift, since it gives substantial engine decompression over reasonable distances. The key is timing your entrance speed so that you are just coming off the throttle and engaging the gear in which you now plan to take the curve when you glide toward its entry point.

The best gear through a curve is usually the one that feels best when arriving at the entry point. You have more confidence knowing you're slowing at the right rate of speed and you're in perfect control when you transition to throttle roll-on carrying your momentum right on through the curve. If in any doubt, downshift an additional gear or drag your rear brake just before entering, with an emphasis on smoothness.

It is safer to be in a lower gear wishing you were in a higher gear than the converse. Lower gears are almost always better than higher gears through the tighter curves.

I'm a public road rider. As such, I don't think about the concept of "apex" when I'm riding the street. I don't think of "turn-in points," either. These terms come from the racetrack and are not appropriate for the street. The racetrack is a unique environment that is all about repetition. Apexes and the turn-in points on a racetrack are largely fixed and are used over and over and over again during the course of a race. Whereas on public roads, each curve is new and often ridden once. The determining factors for leaning into a curve on a public road are safety and traction, and after that, whether you have opened your view sufficiently that the vanishing point moves farther and farther away from you. Only when the road ahead is clear near or far, do you lean in and start carving the curve.

In summary, once you finally arrive at the entry point of a curve, it should be as if you've already gotten there ahead of time—in your mind. Why? Because you had already anticipated it!

The Entry

If you've done your homework during the approach phase, you will be mentally prepared to enter a curve, since that's usually where the fun begins. Upon entering a curve, there are four critical skills you will need to acquire: Move your head. Scrutinize the pavement. Lean your torso forward and into the curve. Accelerate.

MOVE YOUR HEAD means a number of things. First, turn your head in the general direction of the vanishing point because that's where you're headed. Because we humans are only good for about a 20% lean angle before getting disoriented, cock your head so your eyes remain parallel with the pavement, and finally, lift your chin. This somewhat odd head orientation helps you switch focus between the vanishing point and the pavement as you're leaning through a curve. Your vision feels more natural, since leaning yourself through a curve on a motorcycle is such an unnatural thing to do. Tilting your eyes parallel to the pavement helps prevent a possible loss of balance as well. Turn your head, but be flexible. Keep scanning the pavement for issues of safety and/or fun, but don't lock your head or fixate your eyes on anything in particular through a curve.

As you turn your head, you might loosely think of the face of a clock. Regard the hub of the clock, where the hour, minute, and second hands meet, as being the entry point of a curve. You approach the curve from the six o'clock position on the dial. If the curve is a shallow left-hand curve, call that an eleven o'clock curve. Turn your head to eleven o'clock. If the curve is a 90-degree right turn, turn your head to the three o'clock position. If the curve is extra tight to the left, turn your head to the seven o'clock position. But keep it flexible. Again, don't feel you have to lock your head and your eyes on any one vanishing point. Keep moving your eyes, scrutinizing pavement for issues of traction. Speaking of which…

SCRUTINIZE THE PAVEMENT continually and continuously for issues of fun and safety. Whenever you enter a curve, you're in "the land of double-jeopardy" and in possible danger of low-siding. This is what most riders fear. Let factual knowledge overcome emotional fear. (F.E.A.R. False Evidence

Appearing Real.) Overcome this fear of low-siding by making sure you are scrutinizing the pavement for details. You must know-that- you-know the pavement and are thus placing your tires on the best possible line across it. *Knowing* you know breeds confidence! When riders crash, it is often an overblown panic reaction that puts them in the weeds. They panic because they are not paying enough attention as they blissfully lean through the aforementioned curve.

Unlike a race rider, I cannot focus all my vision at the vanishing point while I navigate through an entire curve. My eyes must be flexible. On public roads, I have to divide my focus between both the vanishing point and the pavement directly in front of me. The latter is more important than the former. First, I must be scrutinizing that pavement immediately ahead of me for issues of safety, camber, and traction; only then can I move on to the vanishing point.

On the racetrack, motorcyclists can focus almost exclusively on the vanishing point because they have the relative luxury of being able to take traction for granted. Decent traction throughout is what they're paying for! Street riders should be so lucky.

LEAN YOUR BODY. Much has been written and taught about leaning your body through a curve. Most of this seems to come from racers who have become public road instructors. Many of them emphasize the importance of leaning your torso into the curve. My technique is different, and not much written about, but it does come from several hundred thousand miles riding mountains safely. I don't emphasize leaning your torso much into a mountain curve. What I *do* emphasize is leaning your torso farther *forward* through a curve. What a public road rider wants through curves is maximum confidence. Maximum confidence is what's achieved by learning to lean your torso farther *forward*. Only then do I also slant my torso slightly into the curve, as needed.

ACCELERATION. Have you ever ridden through a curve and felt so planted that it was as though your machine was locked on rail? Acceleration, whether intentional or not, gives you that effect. That's right, it's the secret sauce that gives you the thrill! Acceleration keeps momentum and weight back on the rear wheel where it belongs, steadying the rear suspension in its "sweet spot" center of its travel. The key is to have just enough pressure on the throttle, rolling on millimeter by millimeter, to maintain acceleration throughout a curve. The slightest acceleration is all it takes to lock onto the rail. If you want to accelerate faster, do it; just be safe, and keep moving your eyes as you enjoy the thrill! All of this is possible if you've set up the curve correctly on the approach with the proper entry speed that allows you to then accelerate.

In the Curve

If you've done your homework during the approach and entry phases, being in the curve follows naturally. The idea is to hold your momentum, stay on your planned line, and continue gradually accelerating.

Assuming you're leaning forward and making subtle course corrections as needed by counter-steering or adding throttle, try sitting as still as possible. Less is more. Take a survey of your inner self as you're leaning to make sure you are not clenching anything other than the tank with your thighs. Stay relaxed. Breathe. Get out of your own way and let your motorcycle do its job. Keep your eyes moving. Evaluate the pavement surface at the vanishing point and anticipate what the vanishing point is going to do next.

In a tightening curve, the vanishing point will move in closer. It will move faster, too, approximating the speed that you are traveling. In very tight curves, pavement study is at the vanishing point, because it's now very close and there is no room or time to move your eyes elsewhere. As you'd expect, this takes practice, so take it easy. Ride at speeds that keep your focus sharp. It's a balance. Don't ride so fast that you miss relevant details, but don't ride so slowly that you miss those same details because you've become bored or distracted.

I had a rider in the Workshop once who busted wide through a garden-variety curve and wound up bumping into somebody's front yard. I asked him afterward what the heck he was thinking. He told me his mind was on his upcoming Bahamas vacation! He was so distracted by his vacation plans that when the curve appeared, he didn't have the presence of mind to respond. "What! Your mind was in the Bahamas??" I told him if anything, his mind should have been focused as if on a Broadway stage: The curve is "showtime!" Full concentration is demanded when navigating a curve.

Another time, I was riding with a fellow who is a locally-known artist recognized for his paintings of cityscapes. We were riding along the Blue Ridge Parkway a few miles south of the James River. The Parkway rolls along peacefully here for about five miles. For most sport-tourers, it's a middle-to-high gear stretch of road. Then, abruptly, the road curves tightly left and starts climbing to its highest elevation in Virginia. While the curve is sudden, signage marked it for caution. Instead of simply leaning left and carving the curve, this rider rode off the road for no apparent reason. A tow-truck was even needed to winch his bike out from a gully. His year-old expensive Italian sport-tourer with its fancy exhaust was totaled, and he suffered multiple bruises and a concussion. He earned himself an "F" for anticipation too. He later mentioned something about his throttle suddenly accelerating. Perhaps. It's more likely that he was overwhelmed by the Parkway's scenery and simply not paying attention. Suddenly, when the curve appeared, he was startled and his throttle hand froze. Let me repeat: "Showtime" concentration is called for when navigating a curve, especially mountain curves.

Then there are experienced riders who motor along just fine on open roads—until they approach a low-gear curve. Then, if these riders can't see ahead to their satisfaction, they slow down to a relative crawl, creating a disruptive bottleneck for any riders behind them. Of course, these apprehensive riders assert their caution by pointing out that there just might be a hazard on the backside of the curve, and they want to be safe. The real issue is F.E.A.R. and/or they lack the skill to better deal with the shorter sight lines of curves and hill crests other than to dramatically slow down. Why? Because, consciously or not, they have chosen not to improve their visual skills, or they are distracted by entertainment in their headsets or preoccupied by their wandering minds. I see ridership deteriorate around curves all the time.

Be in a mindset of expecting the unexpected, because hazards are going to appear. Expect them! But most hazards never magically appear, especially if they are stationary or slow moving. It's never "Presto!" and out of nowhere, a malevolent hazard pops up in front of you. Hazards don't appear like that. Instead, they appear progressively like the Peterbilt, or a farm tractor. If you're expectantly watchful, even something as small as a brick will always progressively appear at the vanishing point on a hill crest—presenting itself from its top, down through its middle, and on down to the pavement, or around a curve—from its near side, through its middle, to its far side. If you've seen this brick as it first presents itself (like a small wafer on the horizon,) you're going to have plenty of time to avoid it. On the other hand, if you are obliviously winding your way around a curve, rocking away in your headset, or with your eyes or mind elsewhere, all of a sudden - POW! Call it for what it is: Pilot error.

To a small degree, your throttle can alter your line. For example, if you need to tighten your line while you're leaned in, roll off your throttle just a bit or drag your rear brake. The bike will fall in, automatically tightening your line. Arrest this by applying opposite counter-steer or by gently goosing the throttle. Either way, the bike will stand up, thus widening your line.

Winding through successive curves is an ideal time to take your commune with your motorcycle to a higher level. Tighten your thighs against your gas tank to establish a firm grip, and then try using your hands in a way that perhaps you had not considered before. Don't just change your grip - actually release your grip. That's right! Lean and rest your open hands on your handgrips using the "V" between your thumb and index finger; relax, and go with the flow. By relaxing your grip (little by little) you will be able to truly feel the motorcycle and your body's influence on it through the handlebars like you've never felt it before. You want to use your whole body as a "sensation detector" to probe deeply into the center of your machine all the way to the pavement. Feel!! Strive to feel your body's influence on the quality of your motorcycle's leaning. Strive to feel your momentum. Work with it. Control the smoothness of your acceleration and deceleration. No herky-jerkiness on the throttle. Make smooth transitions to sharpen your line. Continuous precision makes for a sharp, smooth line. After all, when you thread a needle, aren't you being continuously precise? It takes a smooth hand to thread a needle.

When flying in zero visibility and setting up to land the airplane, air traffic controllers would occasionally ask my exact position. If I told them I was "on the needles," it was understood that I had situational awareness and had centered my airplane precisely on two specific radio beacons—the localizer (for horizontal precision) and glide slope (for vertical precision) in a controlled descent. Showtime! By continuously centering the instruments' needles on those beacons in zero visibility, I would touch my airplane down on the center line of the runway. My tolerance for error was no more than the width of the instrument needles themselves. When you ride the curves, make sure that you too are "on the needles."

Exiting the Curve

Before you know it, you are exiting a curve. You know that you are moving out when the vanishing point rapidly outpaces you only to settle somewhere else down the road.

On the other hand, if you are engaged in a series of S-curves, the vanishing point is going to move in the opposite direction of your lean. Precise positioning as you exit one curve ought to set you up precisely for the next curve. For example, if you're leaning through a right curve, lean in tight in the right mini-lane, taking the shortest distance around the curve. As the curve opens up and transitions into a left curve, you're already placed in the correct mini-lane for the clearest right-to-left view through the upcoming left-hander. The same thing applies going around a left curve. Try to hold your line tight to the right, seeing through the left curve; if things look good, stay there, for the shortest line again through the upcoming right curve.

A series of S-curves is just like a beautiful score of music—the beauty is in its details. Pay attention to them. The curves will then reward you with the best times of your ride, and the "score" will remain in your mind long after—or at least until you saddle up the next time and ride away.

There you have it. Four key skills to embrace whenever you carve a curve: Move your head. Scrutinize the surface. Lean your body; Accelerate through the curve.

Leaning a Motorcycle

More seems to have been written about leaning a motorcycle through a curve than just about any other motorcycling skill. It's easy to understand why. For one, leaning a motorcycle is what gets the machine to turn. It's also the most enjoyable and confidence-affirming skill a motorcyclist can have—when done the right way. Conversely, leaning a motorcycle through a curve can be the most miserable, confidence-shattering experience a rider can have—when done the wrong way. The choice is yours.

The problem is that learning to lean the machine is not exactly intuitive.

To lean a motorcycle, you need to do two things nearly simultaneously: You must counter-steer to get the motorcycle to lean, and you must lean a bit of yourself too.

At anything above about 15 mph, steering a motorcycle in motorcycle parlance is called "counter-steering", and it's the part that isn't intuitive because things are done oppositely. To steer left, push the left handlebar clock-wise. Notice that the front wheel effectively turns to the right. But the bike will immediately lean to the left and soon thereafter start to turn to the left. To counter-steer right, push the right handlebar counter-clockwise as if you are turning the front wheel to the left. The bike will lean right and turn right. It's all opposite, but that's counter-steering!

But counter-steering alone isn't quite enough to steer a motorcycle. You must also lean your torso, and you lean two ways! You lean your torso farther forward than you would in straight-road riding and you lean slightly into the direction that you are turning. I call this combined leaning "body-English" and it's all a matter of degree. The practice of counter-steering plus "body-English" is the fusion of three skills that gets the motorcycle leaning precisely and safely through the turn.

It's important to keep in mind that counter-steering alone is the predominant method by which to steer a motorcycle. "Body-English" simply makes the turning process easier and more natural. On the other hand, some motorcyclists firmly believe that a motorcycle is turned by the rider shifting almost all of his weight and dramatically leaning. What settled the issue for me was a video circulating on the Internet showing a motorcycle equipped with two sets of handlebars. One is the stock set; the other is a set of fixed handlebars welded onto the frame itself. In the video, riders are asked to ride down a non-functioning airport runway using only the welded handlebars for steering. The objective was to turn the bike through several widely-spaced highway cones using "body-English" alone. It couldn't be done. None of the riders was able to steer the motorcycle to any useful degree. However, when riders tried again using only the factory-equipped handlebars, all went well. So, to steer a motorcycle anytime, anywhere, I suggest you initiate the steering by counter-steering and simultaneously follow through with "body-English" for easier steering as needed.

Counter-steering is relatively easy once you get the hang of it. The confusion lies in how to apply "body-English," since there are actually two ways to lean your body.

The method I suggest for applying "body-English" through a curve on a public road (as opposed to the racetrack) is to first exaggerate leaning your torso farther forward on the saddle and only then lean your torso into the curve as needed. This works especially well on tighter and slower first, second, and third gear curves—not so much on fourth, fifth and sixth gear curves since you're not needing to lean the bike much in such gradual turns.

Something rather profound happens when you lean your being far forward. You feel better! You feel more confident. With the balls of your feet parked on the foot pegs, your thighs gripping the gas tank, lean your torso farther forward than you usually do—about 35 to 45 degrees, or enough to bring your chest closer to the tank. Relax your elbows to the extent that gravity drops them down toward your knees. Use your arms to shock absorb your torso. The "look" is a little like a jockey sitting on a racehorse. In fact this position is similar to any number of "sporting postures." Bicyclists winding through curves are all leaning forward, elbows bent; wrestlers are crouched with torsos forward, knees bent, arm out with elbows bent; so are practitioners of martial arts. Keeping your body low and light on the balls of your feet, arms out and elbows bent, is a common human position for being physically at the ready—for action!

Leaning far forward has several benefits. For one, your center of gravity is shifted forward and down, providing more grip to the front tire. Leaning farther forward with more bend in your elbows also provides better road feel and control. Yet there's more: You will feel more confident! Start by exaggerating your forward lean in order to get the full effect. Develop an awareness for the full effect of this sporting posture. With time, you'll settle into the more subtle forward position that works best for you, and it won't need to be as exaggerated.

Motorcycling is about managing risk and managing your survival instincts when sudden risk occurs. Whenever we experience a risky moment, our natural survival tendency is to push away by clenching the grips and stiff-arming the handlebars. Stiff-arming locks your means of control. Stiff-arm your handlebars through a technical curve and you'll find yourself in the bushes! The better response is to quickly lean far forward whenever an "Oh sh*t" moment is felt. Train yourself to lean far forward through all curves and/or any time you feel tense. Do it to different degrees based on the situation. To develop leaning farther forward into habit, lean farther forward while accelerating; lean farther forward while braking; lean farther forward while simply motoring down the road. Good things happen when you lean forward, and better things happen when you lean farther forward. Instantly you will have "can-do" confidence and better control. Try it! You'll be glad you did! When a ride suddenly becomes risky, I'd rather being sitting forward like a jockey on a racehorse than slouching like a sack of potatoes any day!

Leaning your upper torso forward through a curve is the primary lean angle to adopt, but subtly leaning your torso *into* a curve will facilitate your ability to lean the motorcycle over into those more exciting second, third, and fourth gear curves. I call this side-to-side lean technique the "pelvic tilt."

Think about entering a left-hand curve. As you counter-steer to the left, simultaneously lean far forward and slightly off-weight your outside (right) pelvic bone, tilting your pelvis sideways down and to the left. This presses your left buttock into the seat. As you do, relax. Breathe. Allow your torso to sag left rather than actually lean to the left. Leaning your torso forward should be exaggerated, at least initially; sagging your torso into a curve shouldn't be. The leaning motion is subtle. Remember: The goal is to exhibit an economy of movement. Effortlessness. As you sag left, feel the motorcycle as it is leaning in and take note of the experience. Notice you do not have to apply as much handlebar counter-steering pressure as you otherwise would. If you were to carefully relax your grip, you would see that the motorcycle would continue leaning all by itself.

Everyone's body mass distribution is different, and everyone's motorcycle is set up slightly differently. Some of us carry our weight in our upper body, while others carry weight down low. Some people own motorcycles with upright seating positions and wide handlebars, while others own motorcycles with more lean-over go-fast positions and narrower bars. For those who carry weight down low or have narrower handlebars, you'll likely have to apply more inside body lean. Try pressing your outside thigh against the tank as you're doing it. Press firmly. See if doing so assists in leaning the bike. The point is to determine what leaning position/technique works for you. The goal is to make leaning your motorcycle into a curve as easy and as natural as possible. Lean far forward. Lean a little less. Push harder on the inside handlebar. Push a little less. Tilt your pelvis more. Tilt it less. Determine how best these various rider positions work for you. After all, you are the boss of both your body and the beast!

As I've mentioned before, keep your eyes parallel with the pavement. If you are leaning your body to the left, tilt the top of your head slightly up and back to the right. By tilting your head in the opposite direction of your lean angle, your eyes stay parallel with the pavement and you minimize the likelihood of losing your balance or becoming disoriented, especially if you're steep-leaning through the curve.

Steep-leaning a motorcycle through a curve on a public road, while a lot of fun, can lead some to think that literally hanging the body off the motorcycle through the curve is even more fun, not to mention looking pretty cool. The idea of hanging the body off the motorcycle comes directly from the racetrack. Motorcycling enthusiasts are thrilled to watch racers hanging off their bikes on TV during every race, through each and every corner. What works on the racetrack must surely work on public roads, right? Here is the point of "hanging off": The sole objective of the racetrack rider is to maintain maximum overall speed over the duration of the race—bullet-fast on the "straights," and faster than anyone else through the corners. To achieve maximum speed through the corners, racers need maximum traction. Maximum traction in the corners is preserved by reducing the motorcycle's lean angle. To reduce a motorcycle's lean angle, the racer lowers his own center of gravity to the extreme by actually leaving the saddle and hanging most of his body off the motorcycle low and to the inside. The motorcycle is thus able to stay more upright and lose less traction to sidewall forces while maintaining maximum speed.

Leaning a Motorcycle

With the strict rules at the track and everyone's rigid adherence to them, hanging off the bike is relatively safe. Racers are all traveling in the same direction and have memorized each turn and have been through each curve many times over the duration of the race. Even if it's a blind curve, racers have studied and know exactly where the perfect line is, and they make every effort to not deviate from it. Plus, racers know the track surface is completely predictable. Thus, a racer can safely lean his body as much as he wants to preserve traction at the wheels. These racers can go so far off their saddles that they drag knees and even elbows! (Note: True racing tires have a decidedly more "V" profile—narrow through the center and relatively wide, flat sidewalls—so they have a lot more rubber on the road when leaned than we do with our typically very round-profile street tires.)

Leaning far off your motorcycle to any significant degree on public roads is dangerous and off-putting to others sharing the road. To be going so fast that extreme leaning is actually necessary angers the public and is likely frowned upon by the local constable. And, to hang off your bike when you're not going fast is totally unnecessary and, frankly, looks silly. Plus, think about it: When you are hanging off the side of your motorcycle, you are totally committed! Public roads aren't predictable like racetracks. Surface conditions can change from day to day, and mountain road conditions can change abruptly by the hour. Imagine dramatically leaning off your motorcycle through a left decreasing-radius mountain curve only to encounter a wide wash of gravel. I've seen it. Talk about an "Oh sh*t" moment! With your body hung off to any degree at all, you won't have time to return to the saddle, raise the handlebars, and quickly reduce the lean angle. What's your choice? Counter-steer farther left? Bust the centerline into the opposite lane where you might encounter oncoming traffic or a guardrail? Hot-dogging on public roadways is dangerous.

That being said, at some point you are still going to want to start steep-leaning your machine. What is steep-leaning, you ask? It's leaning your motorcycle toward the design limit of your tires and often beyond a rider's comfort zone. Steep-leaning is thrilling to do. It is an important safety skill as well. But if you have never learned to steep-lean, you're not going to rise to the occasion and do it in an emergency when doing so would be the only safe solution. You're going to default to whatever your normal habits are. You can't learn how to steep lean your motorcycle on public roads either. There are too many uncertainties. You learn this special skill at the racetrack where good traction is nearly guaranteed, and everyone sharing the raceway knows the rules for safe riding. At the track, you will become aware of any natural reluctance you have to steeper leaning and learn to overcome it. It's one thing to know that modern motorcycle tires in good condition are capable of exceptional grip on clean, dry pavement. But as with all skills, knowing the skill isn't the same as owning it. By repeatedly riding through the same curves, it will become easier to lean more steeply as you develop confidence and know-how.

Mountain curves are the most exciting curves. But there are some mountain curves that require a separate leaning technique to ride well. These are usually first-gear hairpin curves, others are second-gear curves with lousy traction. Some are incredibly steep, too, and still with lousy traction. The position you adopt for these crazy curves is similar to that used for gnarly dirt or off-road carving. Instead of leaning your torso into the curve, you lean away from it. That's right! The goal is to keep your torso upright at a 90-degree vertical angle with the ground so your weight stays directly underneath you. This posture keeps your body pressing straight down on the tire patch, minimizing the possibility of your tires losing grip and sliding out from underneath and low-siding you.

Obviously, you are going to take your own sweet time through these first and second-gear hairpin curves. For example, as you enter a right hairpin, you are going to enter much more slowly than you otherwise would for normal turns, but you must always keep moving. You stop, you tip over. You are then going to push on your inside right handlebar, extending your right arm away from you. As you do, you will shift your weight away and to the left, extending your right arm even farther. The bike is now going to lean steeply down to the right. As it does, the seat is obviously going to lean sharply right as well. Shift your weight far to the left so your left buttock sits far up and on the left side of the seat. Strive to keep yourself more upright and perpendicular to the road surface. Your right arm should be extended out nearly straight as you push the right bar down and away from you.

This position allows the motorcycle to steeply lean and roll through that tight curve, keeping plenty of weight on top of the tires, maximizing tread and grip on a potentially loose surface. You also are sitting more upright for a more commanding view since that is exactly what you need around these turns. No telling what kind of "bogie" is lying in your path as you come around the curve. Keep your eyes moving and concentrating more on the vanishing point than on what is directly beneath you. Focus on exactly where you want your bike to go. Again—don't stop! Keep moving! This technique is not particularly glamorous, but it gets the job of tight cornering done.

Learning to confidently lean your motorcycle into a turn is just about the most important handling skill a any motorcyclist can master. Happily, the better you get, the more fun you have! There is a direct correlation: Leaning equals fun! Leaning your body while leaning your motorcycle into your favorite curves defines much of the "sport" of sport-touring. In this realm, leaning *is* motorcycling, so learn to do it well. Most mountain riders feel that if the motorcycle isn't leaning, the rider isn't really *riding*—at all.

Managing the Engine and Momentum

Any sport-touring motorcyclist who's honest with himself or herself understands that riding a sport-touring motorcycle is more fun when it's ridden kinda/sorta fast. I call it riding "briskly." But let's be real — it's a euphemism. I like riding fast! There are times when I enjoy scorching a road — or two. NOT that I encourage you. No way! It's dangerous. A not so obvious reason riding fast is dangerous is because our DNA never prepared us to be conveyed through the atmosphere at anything faster than we can achieve when being chased by a sabertooth tiger. Riding a motorcycle at speeds higher than that is naturally euphoric and can easily overwhelm our senses. Without some training, conscious thought and experience, it's a cinch to lose control.

Managing the Engine

It's easy to throttle up a motorcycle: Simply put the bike in gear, twist the wrist and off you go. But what actually happens when the wrist is twisted?

The Art of Riding Smooth

Your motorcycle's engine produces power that is expressed in two metrics — horsepower (HP) and torque (foot-pounds). Horsepower is a measure of the power your engine can generate. Torque is a twisting force that causes rotation. Almost everyone is thrilled by the claimed HP output since HP gives an indication of how fast the motorcycle can go and can thus elicit some bragging rights. But torque is actually much more important to you. Torque is where you "live." Think of torque as the "expression of power" in the moment. More torque means the quicker you accelerate and deceleration. When you lack torque, you suffer slower, sluggish acceleration and nearly non-existent deceleration.

When you twist your throttle wrist, your bike's fuel injector(s), or on older bikes, carburetor(s), feed more fuel into the engine, increasing its speed of spinning. Your engine produces varying levels of HP and torque depending on how fast the engine is spinning internally. That rate of spin is expressed as Revolutions Per Minute (RPM). At idle (somewhere between 800 and 1,200 RPM) an engine is typically at its lowest output of both HP and torque. As you twist the throttle and elevate the RPM, both HP and torque increase until at some point, each reaches its peak output. If you continue to roll on throttle after the point where the engine has reached maximum torque, you will end up with little increase in power output, and you'll just be making more noise. If you reach maximum HP, usually near redline, modern engines have engine governors that will retard ignition to automatically limit RPM so you don't destroy the engine.

Most sport-touring motorcycles are equipped with a tachometer, prominently placed on your dashboard to tell you at what RPM your engine is spinning at any instant. Most motorcyclists just call it "the tach." You will want to use it to determine whether you are operating your engine within its optimum power output. Charts that show torque and horsepower in relation to RPMs are available for most motorcycles, either in your owner's manual or on the Web. The RPM value of maximum torque will vary by make, model and year of manufacture, but find it! It's an important point of reference. The RPM value for maximum torque is usually published under Engine Specifications. It is where your motorcycle engine is at its most responsive engine speed. As you climb in RPMs toward maximum torque, your throttle response will be progressively more sensitive until it finally peaks in throttle sensitivity and acceleration/deceleration power at this specific RPM value.

The RPM spread from where the torque starts to really increase to that where the torque is maxed out is commonly called the "power band." Somewhere within that power band (as identified by the RPMs displayed by the tach) is where you should strive to operate your motorcycle nearly all the time. For example, assume the RPM value for maximum torque is given as being at 7,500 RPMs. Your bike's power band may begin around 3,500 RPMs. So, your optimal power band is roughly between 3,500 and 7,500 RPMs. Power band characteristics can vary considerably by motorcycle model. A motorcycle designed for low-speed, off-road use will have a power band skewed toward the lower RPM range with more torque at lower RPMs and a very flat peak Plateau on the chart. That is what you want for slogging through mud or clambering up hills. The multi-cylinder, short-stroke, high-compression, high-revving racing motorcycle will often achieve its highest power output in the higher RPM range and may have relatively little torque until the engine is spinning at about 6,000 RPM. To achieve optimum performance, investigate and memorize your motorcycle's performance characteristics as documented in the owner's manual or elsewhere, and then get out and experience it.

Pay attention to the bottom and top halves of your motorcycle's power band. The bottom half of the power band (perhaps 3,500-5,500 RPM) generally provides sufficient power for straight and level cruising. The top half of the power band (perhaps 5,500-7,500 RPM) provides optimum power and is where you want to be when you need sporty, instantaneous throttle response to briskly accelerate or decelerate.

Be aware that riding at higher RPMs will incur a bit more fuel consumption. The idea is to balance economy with performance. On open highways and interstates, keep the tach in the lower half of the power band by using your top gear—it is quieter, with less vibration, there is plenty of power, and it's easy on the gas consumption. On the other hand, when sporting over hill and dale in second, third, or fourth gear, the top half of the power band is optimally where you want to be. As a rule of thumb, splitting the difference (hovering between 4000 and 5000 RPM in this example) isn't a bad place for the hypothetical roads that I have been describing. Again, the idea is to have responsive acceleration and deceleration with the most subtle twist of the wrist.

Many riders confuse the "busyness" of a sport-touring motorcycle engine at high RPMs with undue wear and tear on the motorcycle. These same riders avoid revving their engines up high to avoid this perceived high-RPM wear and tear. Nothing could be farther from the truth, although it's easy to understand their concern. Many American motorcyclists grew up driving cars equipped with automatic transmissions, and certainly, the emphasis these days is on fuel economy. Most automatic transmissions tend to briskly get into high gears to achieve this. Motorcyclists often follow suit.

As for the busyness of a motorcycle engine spinning up high, get used to it, because that's exactly what a sport-touring motorcycle engine is designed to do. A sport-touring engine runs better at high RPM than it ever will chugging down low. When you are accelerating, pay attention to the tachometer and, depending on the situation, strive to make as many of your up-shifts after your tach needle is well into the middle of your bike's power band. As you upshift and downshift, try not to cause your motorcycle to lurch. Lurching is hard on your transmission. Make those shifts as smooth as you can.

Finally, an effective way to reduce fatigue from the excessive wind and engine noise of riding a motorcycle is to wear earplugs. I won't ride without them. The eminent 1979 Hurt Report definitively researched and concluded that prolonged motorcycle riding causes hearing loss, so take heed. Riders have told me that when wearing quality earplugs, they ride a gear lower than they do without earplugs. That tells me that riders operate their motorcycles based on their ears rather than by the quality of the engine's performance, which is no way to operate a motorcycle.

Managing Momentum

It's easy to speed up a motorcycle. Now think about what happens when you abruptly chop the throttle. Feel the momentum of your body and motorcycle surge forward as you continue rolling down the road—at ever reducing speeds. What you're feeling is the combined mass of your body and motorcycle which could easily approach one thousand pounds. Once the momentum of your body and motorcycle is built up, it's not so easy to manage it when it's time to slow it down. There are two ways to arrest momentum: By applying the brakes, or by using engine compression. The former is obvious, the latter—not so much. Coasting to a stop doesn't count.

Using your brakes is the surest way to precisely slow your motorcycle or bring it to a stop. Roughly 85 percent of a modern sport-touring motorcycle's stopping power comes from its giant front brake, so when you need it, use it! When you apply the front brake, gently squeeze the brake lever. It's immaterial how dire or panicky your stopping predicament is. Squeeze smoothly!

The objective is to smoothly transition from a faster speed to a slower speed or to bring the machine to a full stop no matter what the circumstances are.

When it is imperative to stop in the shortest possible distance, apply front and rear brakes in tandem. The application of the front brake should be progressively stronger as the stop ensues, while pressure on the rear brake pedal can actually be lightened. The emphasis needs to be on that front brake! As the stop develops, ever more firmly apply the front brakes by progressively squeezing the lever. This is to allow time for the forward momentum of you and the motorcycle to load the front wheel tire patch and create the increased tire grip you need to haul everything to a complete stop. If you grab that front brake too hard too quickly, the weight will not yet have transferred to the front wheel, and it is very easy to lock it into a skid. A locked front wheel is very unstable. It will slide, you will have no steering control, and you'll crash unless it is unlocked immediately! And, since the mass is leaving the rear as it moves forward, the rear wheel is becoming ever lighter as the stop develops and thus less relevant to the stop. Too much pressure on the rear brake pedal will result in locking that wheel. The remedy for a locked, skidding rear wheel is to leave it locked and ride it out. If a locked rear wheel results in a sideward slide, releasing the brake will cause the motorcycle to snap back onto its original path, causing a very nasty crash. However, while disconcerting, a locked rear wheel is nowhere near as dire a problem as a locked front wheel. A locked front wheel almost always results in a crash, it's just a matter of when and how ugly.

Being aware of the massive gripping power of the front brake on my motorcycles, I keep my right index and middle finger over the front brake when I am sport riding. With two fingers, I am pre-positioned. Before I need it, I'm already on the lever. Anticipation, remember?

Again, use the rear brake in conjunction with the front brake. As you squeeze the front brake, press firmly on the rear brake as well. Just don't stomp on it! You are better able to stabilize the bike by having both the front and rear suspension settle equally and not having as much momentum shift to the front. On those same mountain roads, I often have my right heel forward on the foot peg with the ball of my foot hovering above the rear brake in case I need to dab it separately from the front brake.

It's such a good idea to practice the emergency skill of proper hard braking. Go to a large, empty parking lot. Start to roll, gain some speed, and then bring yourself to a hard halt by giving your calipers a meaty squeeze. Again, no grabbing, snapping or stomping, just firm, progressive pressure. Practice again and again emphasizing smoothness until you feel confident that you can overcome the natural survival instinct of jamming on the brakes in an emergency situation. In an emergency situation, you will be so glad you did!

I purposely use my brakes in and around traffic much more than when I am out riding the invisible roads. I want to burn the brake light brightly so that traffic behind me clearly knows my slow-down intentions.

Not so on the invisible roads. With no traffic other than the occasional local, or perhaps the posse I'm riding with, I strive to glide. Engine compression is now my "brake" of choice. The idea is to purposefully stay off the brakes as much as possible. You can challenge yourself this way by putting your best "anticipation" skills to work. Developing this skill will make you a better rider as well as contribute to the look of effortlessness.

Through mostly second- and third gear-curves, the timing of your deceleration makes all the difference in how well you approach the next curve or hill crest. Again, you need to arrive at precisely the right entry speed so you can smoothly transition onto the throttle and idealistically stay on the throttle all the way through the curve or over the hill crest.

Along an undulating road, the rule of thumb for managing momentum is to up-shift on the downhills and down-shift on the uphills. Let your momentum do most of the work; your job is to nudge it along.

As you crest a hill and are likely headed down, you will feel your momentum increase. Up-shift, roll-off, and glide. Let your momentum carry you along. As your speed increases and you're feeling good, up-shift again, turn the engine loose and glide more freely. If you feel any doubt about what lies ahead, go ahead and down-shift! Manage that momentum. Down-shift yet again if you need to. Arrest your steed's speed. When in doubt, down-shift! That's my motto, and I down-shift for all manner of things. Hell, I downshift just for the joy of the shift. And remember this: In a tight curve, lower gears and higher RPM are nearly always better than higher gears and lower RPM. You will have more precise throttle control. Believe it!

As you climb, hold your speed. Without any input, gravity will intervene, and at the very instant you feel your momentum start to slow, down-shift! Feel the resulting increased torque as you now smoothly throttle up and continue nudging your momentum along.

My sister is an accomplished pianist. While not a musician myself, I like imagining my motorcycle as a musical instrument. When I'm in this frame of mind, the road becomes a swinging "musical score," and my passion is to "swing" it as smoothly as I can. Smooth. Always smooth. Those momentum shifts? They are "musical notes." The idea is to shift gears spot-on those "notes," in sync with the road, and rhythmically nudge momentum along.

Swinging your motorcycle down a favorite road is all about smooth transitions. A musician wants his note-to-note transitions to sound smooth and sweet to the ear. A rider wants his riding transitions to be sweet and smooth too. After all, motorcycling smoothly IS a sensory or "seat of the pants" kind of thing—up-shifting and down; rolling on to rolling off to rolling back on again; counter-steering this way and that; braking front and rear - while always being smooth. Especially strive for smooth gear shifts. Super smooth gear shifting is another non-negotiable skill to master if you are to become an expert motorcyclist.

An accomplished musician knows the technique for creating sweet notes. So too, you will want to know the technique for creating smooth shifts—every time. Without developing this specific shifting technique, you'll never truly be smooth, nor will your ride be sweet.

I learned the "art of the shift" from another master motorcyclist when I first attended Reg Pridmore's

C.L.A.S.S. course at the Watkins Glen Raceway in Upstate New York. For a $20 contribution to the Man's favorite charity, I was able to climb on the back of the motorcycle with Reg for a couple of go's around the track. It was on the back of his bike that I first experienced the art of the seamlessly smooth shift. For the life of me, I felt nothing at all! I have personally used Reg's seamlessly smooth shift technique ever since and have taught it in the Workshop from the beginning. Smooth shifting is part of my craft, and nowadays, I consider myself very good, though not yet a master. I am still practicing, still striving for Reg's high bar of seamlessness.

The act of shifting gears involves using the shifter, the clutch and the throttle. Beginners are taught that these three controls are employed simultaneously which is true. I want to add a subtle refinement: Just before the shift, try putting slight boot pressure on the shifter. If you're down-shifting, apply a bit of downward pressure on the shifter. If you're up-shifting, lift up on it a bit - just until you start to feel resistance. Some call this "pre-loading the shifter." Then, in one deft motion, apply just a bit more pressure on the shifter while delicately squeezing the clutch as you modulate the throttle. Voila! The gear shifts quickly and smoothly!

Applying advance pressure on the shifter is a little like water pressing against a door. As soon as the door is cracked, water instantly rushes in. With shifting, it is the same theory. With pressure already being applied to the shifter, even a tiny squeeze on the clutch lever will allow the shift to occur. Your job is to feel for that point, be with it, and then smooth it out. The abrupt sensation is somewhat like what you feel when snapping or unsnapping a fastener on a pair of jeans. There's the sense of the pressure of pushing or pulling on the fastener when it suddenly "snaps!" When shifting, pre-load the shifter with a bit of pressure. You then just squeeze in the clutch and suddenly, "SNAP!" you are in the new gear. The shifter snaps into gear and it happens fast—feeling like a snap snapping. Got it?

To gain the smoothness that you are striving for, feed the clutch back out while modulating the throttle and feel for smoothness. How smoothly you re-engage the transmission via the clutch lever largely determines how smooth the shift will be. Regulate the throttle, too. When down-shifting, rev the engine (blip the throttle) just a tiny bit to match the engine speed to that of the rear wheel, so when you feed out the clutch to re-engage, the now accelerated speed of the engine/transmission matches the faster rear wheel speed. When you are up-shifting, roll off just a bit or hold the throttle steady and coast, so when you feed out the clutch to re-engage, the rear wheel has slowed down slightly to match the slower speed of the engine/transmission. Clutching, shifting and throttling happen in unison. Smooth re-engagement is all about timing and feel, and you're the only one to do it—so practice!

You cannot shift gears too often. Shifting gears is a fundamental motorcycle craft, which reminds me of— Mick Jagger. Years ago, my wife got us tickets to the IMAX presentation of "Ladies and Gentlemen: The Rolling Stones." It was a film documenting the band's 1989 Steel Wheels concert. Before the show, the IMAX crew went backstage and into a warren of small dressing rooms. Here and there on long tables were picked-over containers of food and empty liquor bottles. Roadies and girl groupies milled about, in and out of camera range. In the background was the faint sound of what seemed like—could it be??— yodeling! The camera went farther and deeper into the dressing rooms. There was less din, and soon we were alone. Finally, around another corner, in the far back of a room, was Mick, by himself, intently looking into a mirror. The man was standing there, limbering-up his vocal chords before the show by yodeling up and down musical scales! By this time he had been in the business of rock 'n roll for over 25 years—yet there he was, still practicing the fundamental skills of singing. Why? Because Mick Jagger is a pro, that's why. No wonder the Stones are considered by many the best rock 'n roll band in the world!

Larry Bird, whom some foolishly called a "dumb hick," hailed from French Lick, a crossroad in nowhere, Indiana. As a boy, Bird had aspirations to become a big league basketball star. While in high school, he dedicated himself to shooting 250 jump shots every day of his high school life. In part by mastering this fundamental skill, Bird made it to the highest level of pro basketball. The Boston Celtics retired his number.

For these two masters, Jagger and Bird, the practice of getting better wasn't work at all. Work is "work" only if there's something else you'd rather be doing. Both men loved what they did. For them, practice was fun!

If you aspire to be a great motorcyclist (and why not, since you didn't spend many thousands of dollars on your sport-tourer to remain average, did you?) you really must develop the "art" of the seamless shift. Seamlessness is the high bar. Whenever you're riding "straight and level," just droning along, exercise your transmission's "scales" by repeatedly shifting gears. Take a speed, any speed - for example, 50 miles an hour. Start in your highest gear. Then down-shift. Then down-shift again and down-shift again. Now up-shift and up-shift again and again back into high gear. Do it again. And again. And again. And again. Shift up and down through your bike's gears (being reasonable and depending on speed) and dedicate yourself to making each shift so smooth as to be nearly imperceptible. Another way to practice is to pretend that you have a cup of coffee clutched between your knees. Make each gear transition so smooth that nary a drop of coffee gets sloshed from the cup. There just is no substitute for regular practice with the earnest intent of getting better. But make it fun!

Soon, you are going to become a really smooth gear shifter. Precise throttle control at critical times during a ride makes for safety and fun, and there is no better way to achieve throttle control than by measured shifts, one shift after another, until you're precisely where you need to be. If possible, no brakes! Strive for an effortless look.

I usually aim to drop into my chosen gear in the final few yards of the approach, just prior to the entry point of a mountain curve. I've "needled" my speed. Then, in fluid motion, I transition from throttling down to throttling up through the entire length of the curve. Some riders drive hard on the throttle well into the curve racetrack style, and then go hard brakes in the middle of the turn. That gets the job done but the look isn't of effortlessness Other, journeymen riders have the habit of blasting on the straights as I've mentioned before, only to creep through the curves. Polished riders take it easy on the straights only to accelerate swiftly and somehow magically disappear around the curves because, like Mike the "new guy," that's how "the art of riding smooth" is done!

Here's a useful skill: There are going to be times when approaching and leaning through a curve demands even more refinement of momentum, and dropping a gear won't solve it alone. This skill works best when you are deliberately approaching a curve a little hot, climbing or descending, it doesn't matter. When you feel conditions are ripe, and the curve is just moments away, stay in your present gear and firmly apply both front and rear brakes. Get down to a speed that feels right. Now, for some zip, keep the rear brake firmly pressed and smoothly begin releasing the front. With the rear brake still firmly pressed, keep it pressed and stay steady on the throttle to "drag" your motorcycle through the curve. By keeping firm and steady pressure on the rear brake and applying an offsetting steady or increasing throttle against that pressure, your bike will feel more stabilized and controlled around the curve. If you want more speed, release some of the pressure on the rear to let the bike "drag" a little freer; if you want to go slower, simply press the brake pedal a bit harder. This technique works especially well in sharper curves, both ascending and descending - the sharper and steeper the curve, the better it works for you. On stretches of iconic East Coast twisties like Rt. 129's "Dragon" at Deals Gap, NC or Rt. 421's "Snake" at Shady Valley, TN or up north on Smoke Hole Road south off Rt. 55, west of Petersburg, WV, this skill is a sharp arrow in your quiver of skills and will put you in very good shape indeed anytime you are curve-carving and need a little something extra.

Another place where rear braking is apropos is anywhere that low speed is required. Everyone knows that slow rolling in first gear is herky-jerky. Here's how to smooth out first gear maneuvering: Be in first gear and apply sufficient throttle to keep the bike moving. No matter what, keep the throttle steady-on. Then, control speed by using a combination of feathering the clutch and applying rear brake. There is a macrocosm of feel when you work the clutch lever within the friction zone. It's that delicate hand movement where you are partially engaged—a tad more squeeze of the clutch and you're reducing power to the rear wheel—or ease out the clutch lever a bit and you're applying more. Using the friction zone of the clutch like that along with delicate application of the rear brake allows you to tease out a super slow and steady maneuvering speed.

Some might be concerned with wear and tear on the motorcycle clutch doing all of this friction-zone dragging. Certainly, when feathering a wet clutch, there isn't any concern for wear and tear at all—not with what we are discussing here. And, even with a dry clutch, at such low speeds and short duration, there isn't really any concern, either, since little destructive heat is generated. Like anything else, to develop skill with this slow speed technique, find yourself a parking lot or, better yet, find a hard-packed, dry, grassy field to practice on. When it comes to managing momentum, either slow or fast, there is no substitute for regular practice with the earnest intent of getting better.

Whenever I ride a motorcycle, I practice getting better. I'm striving to feel a certain feel and to look a certain look. The feel is smooth, and the look is one of effortlessness. Both are described in this excerpted rider review I received not long ago:

"It really is more fun when your speed has increased significantly and others just can't figure out how you can go that fast and make it look so easy. The better I ride, the more fun it is. As an example of this, I was riding home from my last Workshop through some of the great twisty roads in southeast Ohio, when I drove past a service station with two riders milling about—both on late model, powerful European motorcycles. I was going to stop for fuel but decided to push on and stop in another 40 or 50 miles. A little way down the road, the two guys tucked in behind me and we became a nice, tight unit out for an afternoon ride. Not too many miles ahead we entered some of the best curves in southeast Ohio, and that was the last I saw of them until I stopped for gas. They pulled up next to me and one of them said, 'We saw you go by us on a GS like mine and decided we were going to have some fun and show you how real riders handled in the corners. But frankly, you embarrassed us. There was absolutely no way we could stick with you. How did you learn to ride that fast, so well?'"

"'First of all,' I said, 'I recently got trained.' Of course, I gave them your brochure and told them to do themselves a favor and spend a couple of days with you. I then gave them a big smile and said, 'Do you want to tag along until the next fun section and I drop you?'" They joined in as I rode on, completely smiling, alone with my thoughts, but it wasn't long before I pulled away and disappeared." (Ken D., Rochester, New York)

***

Finally, let me leave you with this observation before moving on to a flying story that signaled the pinnacle of my flying career, but applies as well to motorcycling...

My observation is that all of us who are passionate about motorcycling as a craft are on "the journey" toward getting better. No rider is better or worse. Some are just farther along a continuum in the genre of motorcycling they have chosen. I would advocate, however, that the genre of mountain riding is the most challenging and exciting kind of motorcycling there is. The skills required to mountain ride are the most comprehensive skills a street-rider can own.

Putting It All Together

I am reminded of a particular Angel Flight mission I did when inclement weather kept most general aviation pilots grounded. The flight was my second mission for a patient whom I'll call Brian. Earlier in the week my first mission had been to fly Brian from his home in Galax, Virginia to BWI airport near Baltimore. The first time I laid eyes on him at Twin Counties airport (HLX) near Galax, he wore a peculiar mask. It looked as if he had suffered a nasty burn. Practically his whole face was covered. I asked what happened, and he told me that two years earlier, he caught some fragments of an RPG round in Iraq. How horrible! The charge blew away his chin, his lips, his front teeth, his nose, and grazed both his forehead and ear. I felt sick, and could sense right away that he was weary—weary of the pain, weary of the loss of normal routine, and psychologically burdened by the impending surgery he was to undergo in a few weeks. Brian had gained some notoriety in the national newspapers and would ultimately go on to become the first face transplant patient. Pretty amazing! Ultimately, after multiple surgeries, his face was "restored" very satisfactorily.

When Angel Flight gave me patients so sick, wounded or weary, whose bone-tired fatigue was so obviously etched across their faces, I'd often ask if they wanted to sit up front with me and plug into the plane's radio/intercom. They could listen and maybe learn a bit about what flying a small airplane was like. My fascination with aviation ran deep, and it often does with others as well. Sitting "copilot" was an effective distraction for the patients, plus there was always a stupendous front seat view to enjoy. I got Brian plugged in up front for that first flight, and he enjoyed it immensely. Once I had him buckled in and got his headset adjusted, I asked if I could see his face. He looked surprised but then removed his mask, turned and looked at me. Wow! I was so impressed with the courage and forbearance of this young man, and I told him so. He looked slightly skeptical but then smiled and commented quietly that no one outside his circle of comrades, his family and his medical team had ever before asked him to remove the mask. He seemed relieved. He put the mask away, and we totally hit it off. I told him I was honored to be his "chauffeur."

My second mission was to return Brian home from Baltimore. It was a gloomy late January afternoon. When I arrived at my local airport, I parked the car next to the plane, which was tied down and covered in its allotted tie-down space just off a taxiway, behind a row of hangers, out of the wind. I always kept my plane covered when it wasn't being used. I had a ritual for uncovering and covering the plane just so, and I was into that ritual when a fellow pilot wandered by. We chitchatted a moment, and as he stared at the clouds, he remarked how stormy and dangerous the skies seemed. He looked concerned and asked, "You're not really going to be flying today, are you?" The clouds did in fact look ominous. They were obviously heavy with moisture. But I knew the weather wasn't convective or stormy. I just smiled and continued uncovering the airplane.

I had already made a call to Air Traffic Control's Flight Service and had spoken with a dedicated aviation meteorologist. I gave the specialist my name and airplane's "N" number and filed my flight plan. He then proceeded to give me a detailed forecast for my specific route of flight. There was a temperature inversion over the Eastern Seaboard calling for unseasonably warm temperatures at altitude all along my route, and there was no icing predicted to 20,000 feet. There were no recent "pi-reps" or pilot reports of icing, either. That was good. I had experienced extreme icing some years before when a sudden buildup of clear ice on the airplane's leading surfaces forced me to divert to the nearest airport, so I knew something about the perils of icing. I was most pleased that ice would not be an issue as I would be flying at just 11,000 feet. The forecast did, however, call for instrument meteorological conditions or in pilots' parlance, I.M.C. That's when a pilot likely has zero visibility and flies solely by reference to instruments. Plus, most of the flight would be over mountainous terrain and at night as well. I knew I would have to be on my toes.

I took off from my home airport and was soon touching down at BWI airport and taxiing over to the General Aviation depot. I always felt like such a small fry taxiing among the heavier metal on the tarmac.

Brian was in the passenger lounge waiting for me. He had his mask on. I knew he had been at Johns Hopkins Hospital for a series of precise measurements of his face in preparation for his upcoming surgery. After greeting each other and chatting briefly, we walked out to the airplane, climbed aboard, and buckled ourselves in. He pulled his mask off, stowed it, then asked for a headset and plugged in. It wasn't too long before ground control cleared us to taxi, and soon we were next in line for departure. The airliner just ahead of us was a Boeing 777. His call-sign was suffixed with the word "Heavy." This indicated to me and other pilots that there would be dangerous wake turbulence if we were to climb through his departure slipstream. One time, at 7000 feet, over Teeterboro Airport outside NYC, I had flown through a commuter jet's wake turbulence. It shook the hell out of the airplane. So I knew to stay clear. When I was given the authorization for takeoff, I radioed tower control that I was rolling, pushed the throttle forward and lifted off into smooth air well before the preceding jet's takeoff point.

Before long, departure control cleared us to our destination airport. Soon, late afternoon turned to dusk, and as we leveled off at 11,000 feet, nightfall settled in. My trusty bird droned on. All the flight instruments were "needled" with the GPS and backup navigation radios tuned to Brian's destination airport. At some point on the climb, I flipped the switches to fire up the plane's strobe system. Immediately, the cockpit was awash in flashing light as if there was lightening striking all around us! Unbeknown to me, since it was too dark to see, we had entered the clouds and my strobes were bouncing crazy light off the clouds. So much for the strobes; I quickly switched them off.

In the straight and level phase of a night flight, especially flying blind, pinpoint accuracy of the needles is important for situational awareness. My personal margin of error was now the mere width of the needles alone. Once we got about 20 miles north of Roanoke, I radioed ahead to HLX on the number two radio (the number one radio being tuned to air traffic center control) to listen to its automated weather broadcast. Unfortunately, the broadcast called for wind at 10 knots, rain, ceiling less than 200 feet and less than a quarter mile of visibility. I told Brian the weather conditions at Galax were below my "flight minimums" thus precluding our landing there. My flight plan's backup airport was Roanoke. Its weather broadcast called for a much better 1000-foot ceiling and a half-mile of visibility. I said we would have to land there. Brian took that news in but after a few moments asked whether it would be possible to instead land at Blue Ridge Airport (MTV). That would be a lot closer to his mother's place than Roanoke, and his wife could pick him up there the following day. I radioed ahead to MTV to check on their weather. The automated voice broadcast came back reporting a ceiling of 400 feet with broken clouds, winds 6 knots, mist, and a half-mile of visibility. I told Brian I'd make one attempt to land at Blue

Ridge but if we couldn't do it, we'd have to fly back to Roanoke. He was fine with that.

A low ceiling, night mountain landing in mist and rain is as challenging a landing as any pilot can have. I took stock of myself. Was I ready? I was actually remarkably calm—no sweaty hands—and quite eager to make the attempt. I radioed Center for clearance and about 50 miles out of Blue Ridge Airport, they turned me over to Greensboro (NC) Approach Control. It was a shared frequency, so Brian and I listened as an airplane ahead of us tried to land at Blue Ridge. After two attempts to shoot the approach, that pilot gave up and flew elsewhere. I knew then that I'd have to fly my best if we were to succeed in safely making it to the ground given such marginal conditions. I pulled from my pilot's bag the specific charts (called approach plates) for landing at Blue Ridge. The landing touchdown altitude was around 2500 feet above sea level. I knew my approach altitude needed to be 1000 feet above that, or 3500 feet, and the altitude for landing straight-in was 400 feet above touchdown altitude, or 2900 feet. Soon, I radioed Greensboro Approach that I was ready for the approach. They gave me permission to change to that airport's "UNICOM" or local frequency, and requested that I notify them when I had safely landed.

We were now about 15 miles out from Blue Ridge at 7500 feet of altitude. I continued listening to the local weather on a tape-loop droning in the background and broadcasted my intentions to any aircraft in the area. I then eased the throttle back, trimmed the elevators to approach/descent speed and carefully descended the airplane to 3500 feet. I then turned and set the plane up on the exact course heading to intercept the runway threshold. At this point, as matter of procedure, I switched on my landing lights, but all it did was reflect back distracting light into the cockpit so I shut the lights off and told Brian to keep a lookout for any ground lights (street lights, headlights, houselights, outdoor lights, parking lot lights or otherwise) to help orient me as we got closer. MY job was to stay on the needles! Brian continued to advise that he saw no lights. It was as if the entire canopy was painted black.

I was now spot-holding 2900 feet of altitude with a super-precise course heading, continuously correcting for wind and changes in altitude. The ceiling was still 400 feet, no lights were visible on the ground, and I was now just a mile and a half from touchdown. I could tell Brian was anxious. Then I said, 'Hey Brian, check this out!" In a flash, I pressed the radio transmit button five times in rapid succession. Click-click-click-click-click. Instantly, through the murk bright lights and soon the runway environment presented itself in all its flood-lit glory. Yea! With that, I immediately transitioned from approaching the runway to a rapid final descent for landing by easing back the throttle a little more, deploying full flaps, trimming the elevators for final approach speed and, most importantly, transitioning my eyes from having been trained on flight instruments for three hours to now looking outside the cockpit canopy. Showtime! I knew the length of the runway was generous so was certain I could descend through the thin layer of cloud with pavement to spare. Soon the runway threshold appeared ahead and clear enough to touch down—and I did indeed, with my signature "eek" wheeled landing. Brian and I fist-bumped, and I personally gave myself a mental pat on the back for a well-executed 15-mile approach-to-touchdown—even though the whole experience seemed over in the blink of an eye.

Here's the take-away: At no point during this technical landing was I apprehensive. While not a cake walk, I knew I would (not could) land safely. And the fact is, I did not even have to think much about what I was doing. I had trained for this. My reflexes had been honed to such an extent that the entire process of landing the airplane was almost effortless. I had fused with the airplane and during the final landing phase of the flight felt very much that I had entered "the zone" where time and space become one. Truth be told, I had become a more evolved aviator than the pilot I had met earlier that afternoon at my local airport while I was preparing my plane.

Motorcycling is the same: If you take to heart the skills presented in this book and dedicate the seat time to practice so the skills become second nature, you are going to develop into one hell of a motorcyclist. You will also come to fully appreciate the virtues of motorcycling's "Beautiful Paradox" and use it to your advantage and enjoyment.

There's going to come a time for you, too, when other riders are going to ask themselves how in the world you glide so smoothly. You are not going to tell them you are more evolved, although you are. Instead, you're going to tell them that it's from *regular practice with an earnest intent to get better.* Good luck!

The Art of Riding Smooth

In the first chapter of the book, I mentioned that anticipation and precision are my "thing." They are and always will be. I believe that these two skills come from the analytical side of the brain. There is a third skill, however, that I have also mentioned numerous times, and still it deserves mentioning one last time—smoothness—which seems to come from the more creative side of the brain.

Obviously, smoothness is impossible without exercising anticipation and plenty of precision. But being smooth in what we do also requires a keen sense of motion. And aren't we in motion 100% of the time we are riding? The objective, then, is to infuse each control input with all the smoothness our sensitivity to motion can muster.

Our sense of smoothness isn't so much intellectualized, though, as much as it is felt. So be sensitive. Feel deeply. Relax and allow yourself to become smooth. It will come.

I mentioned how easy it is to accelerate a motorcycle, and how it is not so easy to slow one down. To prepare yourself for "the zone" or what I truly believe is a meditative state where "the zone" resides, a rider must endeavor to take his skills to an even higher level—and remain there. To reach this plateau, strive to apply smooth engine-braking when arresting your sport-tourer's speed, especially approaching curves. That's right! This requires that you become a master down-shifter.

Smooth engine braking requires more concentration than traditional wheel-braking. It requires keen anticipation of the right gear and needle-like precision for timing the shift to nail the right entry speed at the right moment. Indeed, it's all about timing! You want to be able to down-shift on a dime, anywhere, any time. Your whole being is now focused, half on the desire for analytical safety (the raison d'être of the mantra) and the other half on artistic smoothness. This focus stills the mind and allows you to create your own "Art of Riding Smooth."

There is something transcendent as you journey toward seamlessness. Your mind performs preternaturally as you glide hither and yon over vast stretches of invisible roads —and it will all seem so *easy*! It's not cockiness. It's confidence! After all, you have practiced until you have gotten it right. Plus, you have continued to practice until you just can't get it wrong! Then, as if by magic, you will enter a special place—a place where time and distance compress into the very still moment of NOW. You've induced "the zone," a sustained intensity that can only be described as ecstasy. The vanishing point beckons you.

THE ART OF RIDING SMOOTH

Reality streams toward you in slow-mo. Then, poof! Your motorcycle disappears beneath you completely. In that forever moment, it's just the eternal you—and you are flying!

The Magical Mountainous Tour

(Step right this way!)

On the journey toward getting better, quantity miles are not the same as quality miles, not that there is anything wrong with quantity miles. High-mileage is often a worthy goal onto itself. But hills and curves must be ridden to develop expert ridership. There is just no escaping it. Motorcycling is very similar to snow skiing in this regard. If a journeyman skier truly intends to get better, he must understand something: He knows what he knows about skiing. Either he knows a lot, or he knows a little. And let's say what he knows, he knows cold. But! That's all he knows. Therefore, if this journeyman skier is wise, he'll seek training from an instructor who knows more. He'll then apply that knowledge and very soon he'll graduate to more advanced slopes. If, during his journey, skiing becomes a passion, our skier is going to continue to develop himself by making the journey to the best ski slopes he can find—somehow, some way. That's passion. It's the same with motorcycling. Riders learn to ride on their local roads. Then, depending on personal interests, they will gravitate to whatever genre of motorcycling they are most attracted to. If mountain riding excites them, they owe it to themselves to discover "Mecca," the Appalachians Mountains.

On the other hand, the reality is that many riders are attracted to touring. In fact, each year, there is a mass migration of riders who are attracted to the vast panoramic views of the Great West and to other scenic regions of the country. But the cinematic, panoramic, technicolor scenery of our Great West seems most appealing of all. I know of riders who have followed the Lewis and Clark, Oregon, and Santa Fe Trails. I know plenty of riders who have made the trek to Alaska and back and who have ridden through all the Western parks as well. All these riders talk about afterward is the beautiful scenery and—that's fine. We all appreciate majestic scenery. But here's my point: The scenic landscape is often observed from afar, often from several miles away. As for the quality of riding, relatively speaking, when compared with riding the vastly underrated hills and curves of the Appalachian Mountains, riding out West doesn't compare! Think about it: The commute to and from, plus the actual riding within each scenic region means hours, if not days, and miles upon miles of whirring in high gears on high-speed roads.

Of course, invariably, there are going to be sections of curvy roads no matter where you ride. But too often, you then have to travel several tens of miles to reach the next segment of curvy roads. Plus many of these curvy roads are engineered and predictable, which can grow repetitive. Back to the snow skiing analogy: Plenty of skiers gravitate to the world-class ski slopes in Colorado and Utah, or Switzerland and Austria. But aren't these skiers there primarily for the quality of the slopes and the actual skiing, and not for the scenery? Admittedly, great slopes wouldn't exist if it weren't for the topography that happens to underpin the scenery. Following the analogy, it seems that most scenic Western motorcycling roads are similar to skiers skiing light-intermediate and "bunny slopes."

As a small example, recently, I was invited to ride the great roads of South Central California. I had earlier met Peter, my host, when he had flown to Maryland from L.A. to join me in a private Workshop. We rode about 750 miles of Appalachian invisible roads over the course of three days. At the end of the ride, we figured we had ridden middle- and low-gear curves for nearly the entire trip. This was a unique riding experience for Peter. Our helmet-mounted Bluetooth communicators emphasized this. What I most remember from that ride was Peter whooping and hollering through the headset, over and over, about what a "goddamn FANTASTIC time" he was having!! (That's how it is when motorcyclists from elsewhere saddle up and ride Appalachian invisible roads.) Afterward, this fine gentleman and high-miler (over 600,000 miles at last count) invited me to his home in Torrance,

California to share some of "his" roads. Since I rarely leave the Appalachians, I took him up on it.

What a host! We rode the canyon roads in and around Ojai. We rode down to Morro Bay. We then rode north along the Pacific Coast Highway up to Monterey. We rode inland to Hollister, then inland south along the infamous San Andreas fault, across the Central Valley to Visalia. We rode the western slopes of the California Sierras, down around Lake Isabella, then up to Lone Pine and through Death Valley. Finally, we rode along both the Angeles Forest and Angeles Crest Highways. There was jaw-dropping scenery everywhere, and that was mostly the point. But the roads themselves were primarily high-gear spinners with a just smattering of middle-gear ones.

It was the same deal with the Ozarks in southern Missouri and northern Arkansas. That region was generously shown to me by Phil, a master guide who knew those roads well. I rode the Ozark Mountains with the intention of creating a Rider's Workshop there. Great scenery. Beautiful wide roads. Fast roads. Nicely- paved roads. All engineered. I experienced one small segment of second-gear curves. True ridership can't be practiced on open roads like that.

The Appalachians, are entirely different. As I have mentioned throughout these pages, it IS possible to stitch together hundreds of miles of low- and middle-gear invisible roads on smooth pavement with practically zero traffic into routes that are truly inspiring from a ridership point of view. These former game trails may not have the jaw-dropping vistas of the West, but the views are scenic just the same. And their continuous curves and smooth, undulating pavement run for miles and miles and miles and miles and miles. THAT'S what is jaw-dropping!

Let me prove it to you: If you think you might like riding mountains, I'd like to share with you an eight-day Appalachian curvy road romp that covers roughly 2000 miles. With little if any traffic! That's right! The route begins in far northeast West Virginia, snug against the Maryland Panhandle. It then extends deeper into northeastern West Virginia, southwestern Virginia and western North Carolina plus a small, but entirely excellent, section of Tennessee for good measure. This route also includes a day or two in two of the best technical motorcycling regions in the country—the Blue Ridge Plateau in southwest Virginia, and Greater Asheville in western North Carolina.

But here's the thing, and it's important: A great motorcycling experience doesn't just happen. Great rides rarely come from skimming a guidebook or highlighting a new map. Instead, great rides require great planning! First, a rider has to be intrigued enough or motivated enough to tackle such an experience. Then, he or she has to plot the route, allocate the resources and finally, make the time to make it happen!

The state of the art in navigation is GPS. The standard in navigation equipment is Garmin Corp. For those who are interested in discovering great riding experiences, investing in a Garmin GPS with turn-by-turn voice navigation is my strong recommendation.

Once you've purchased the GPS and downloaded Garmin's mapping software into both the GPS and your computer, you can purchase the GPS files of my route, hard copy maps, plus a turn-by-by description of my route on my website: www.ridersworkshop.com. Once you have the route package, you will have something that has taken me nearly 20 years to create.

To encourage you to take the plunge, I am going to lay down the gauntlet by declaring this route is the best curvy road mountain ride found anywhere in the United States, if not the world!

I hope you love riding the Appalachian Mountains as much as I have.

Day One: Berkeley Springs, WV to Davis, WV

You heard the joke about West Virginia, right? It's not called the "Mountain State" for nothing. Flatten it out, and it's the size of Texas!

Begin in Berkeley Springs, West Virginia. It's located in the far northeastern corner of the State. Berkeley Springs is a small tourist town once known for its natural geothermal spa. The area was frequented by

Native People. Rumor has it that George Washington took a soak there as well.

I suggest you stay at the Country Inn and dine at Tari's Cafe nearby. I met Tari over 20 years ago. Tari was a big-haired country girl with a dream. She made a real success of her dream and has since retired to sunny Florida, but the quality of her restaurant remains.

Get an early start to begin the adventure by riding Rt. 522 across the Potomac River to Hancock, MD. Exit into Hancock. Get gas at the bright red Sheetz gas station. (My local riding group is the "Between the Sheetz Gang!")

Turn west onto Route 144. Before colonial times, Route 144 was a footpath known by Native People as the Nemacolin Trail. The roadbed is all that's left of this path. That's because it was later converted into the first "road" ever built into the North America wilderness.

It was later renamed Braddock's Road after British General Edward Braddock's army and the engineers who built it. This was in 1755, during the French Indian War, which determined European dominance over North America. The route was built as a "corduroy road," meaning timber was cut and laid crosswise for heavily-laden ox carts full of food, ammunition, medical supplies and other cargo. General Braddock was commissioned by His Majesty, King George II, to sail to Colonial America along with several thousand army regulars. His task was to assemble an army by conscripting local colonists, militia and Indian guides to then trek into the wilderness. Their destination was the confluence of the Allegheny and Monongahela Rivers. Once there, their orders were to subdue the French fort, Duquesne. The fort was erected on the sandy beach between the two rivers at the site of the current city of Pittsburgh. Its mission was to defend French trading interests. It was tall order, and Braddock's army, accustomed to open battle lines, never had a chance. The French and their Native allies, using battle tactics unfamiliar to the traditional British, fired upon them from behind rocks and trees. About ten miles from the fort, the British army was slowly picked off and ultimately defeated. Edward Braddock himself was shot and killed in desperation by one of his own men.

There was an illuminating display of leadership in this debacle, however. A young Virginia militia officer, George Washington, largely saved the day. At all of 23 years old, using exemplary horsemanship and a commanding battlefield presence, Washington led the remnants of Braddock's army in retreat and to relative safety.

You'll notice that Route 144 roughly parallels Interstate 68. By now, I am sure you have ascertained that I'm not much of an interstate rider. Following the ski analogy once again, for my purposes, the interstate is primarily a "chairlift" that expedites me from one region to another and that's all. But often there are interesting roads that parallel interstates. These roads run relatively true and sometimes can even be ridden at speeds close to interstate speeds — not here on 144, though.

Carefully follow Route 144 for 22.7 miles. You will cross over I-68 several times.

Turn left onto Gilpin Road. Follow Gilpin Road through some tight downhill curves to the stop sign. Turn left onto Town Creek Road. Follow the flow of Town Creek Rd. At some point, the road changes names to Bear Hill Rd. Ride a total of 13.5 miles trending downhill to a stop sign at a major road, Route 51. Cross over the road onto what looks like a service road. Follow the road downhill a short distance to where it bends to the right. Ride 0.3 miles.

You are now in Oldtown, Maryland. Oldtown was an old town long before the colonists ever arrived. Oldtown was a major trading center populated by the Native People for decades. It was located here along the Potomac River for two reasons. One was because the river here is relatively shallow. This would allow travois loaded down with trading goods and other supplies, dogs, small children and the elderly to cross the river without fear of being swept away. Not so with horses. Horses were never much part of East Coast Native culture. The second reason is that the north branch and the south branch of the Potomac meet near here to form the Potomac River. Local tribes like the Powhatan and Lenni Linape and Northern tribes such as the Algonquin, Cree, the Six

Nations of the Iroquois, and Huron traded there. So too did Western tribes like the Chippewa, Delaware, Kickapoo, Miami, Mingo, Wyandot, and the ferocious Shawnee. Tribes from the South as well, such as the Cherokee, Creek, Choctaw and even the Seminole all came to trade at Oldtown. They lay down their weapons to barter and trade.

You will see an old stone house in Oldtown with a historical marker in front of it, once owned by the British trader, Michael Cresap. Evidently, he was quite a character and successful trader, but was later loathed by the Native People and accused of murdering an important Mingo chief, Logan, and his family. He died at age 35 of illness while on travels to New York.

Turn left and prepare to lighten your wallet by a 50-cent toll. You're about to cross the privately owned Oldtown Bridge. The toll is for upkeep.

From the far side of the Oldtown Bridge, follow the flow of Greenspring Valley Road/AKA Route 1 0.9 miles under a railroad bridge and across some railroad tracks. Turn left and motor Greenspring Valley Rd. about 8 miles to a stop sign at the bend of Route 28 and Springfield Pike.

Turn hard left onto the smaller Springfield Pike/AKA CR-3, and follow it 6.7 miles along a nice stretch to the next stop sign. You will have traveled alongside the upper Potomac River, and up and over a small mountain.

I have a friend who lives nearby. He has another friend who also grew up around Oldtown and whose family farmed the bottomland along the Potomac in this area. As a farm boy, he unearthed and collected arrowheads and other native artifacts such as a wide variety of arrowheads, clay pots, parts of old flintlocks and even parts of old tomahawks, all of which are assembled into quite a personal collection.

At the stop sign, turn right onto Jersey Mountain Road and follow it 11 miles across open countryside to Route 50. Turn right on Route 50 and ride 1.4 miles. Turn left and start trending farther south on Grassy Lick Road. Follow the flow of Grassy Lick Road 13.1 miles to the next stop sign. Turn right and ride another 5.3 miles through the crossroads of Rio. Grassy Lick Rd. flows into Route 29 and continues another 6.7 miles to Old WV Route 55. Turn right.

Here's the take-away: There ain't no way a rider, other than a local, will ever discover such fine pieces of asphalt as this stretch from the turn onto Town Creek Road up on the Maryland Panhandle, down the long grade to and across the Potomac River at the Oldtown Bridge, and then farther on down to Old Route 55. This is some of West Virginia's best backcountry motorcycling, and it's worth coming from anywhere in our "Lower 48" if motorcycling paved back country roads is what you like to do!

Ride 18.4 miles on Old WV Route 55 (the "Double Nickel") to the T-intersection in downtown Moorefield, West Virginia. Route 55 used to be the main east-west route across this section of West Virginia. Parallel Route 48, which will become an interstate at some point, was built more recently. It's a wonderful thing, too, because the older road has been abandoned by thru traffic. Old 55 is now left to the few locals who live along it and bequeathed to mountain riders like us. Man, life is good!

Turn left and ride 2.3 miles. At the stoplight, turn right on Fisher-Moorefield Road. If you ride past the large "84 Lumber" sign, you will have ridden too far. Ride about 1.5 miles. Just across the North Fork of the Potomac, the road will bend to the left and then bend to the right and proceed uphill onto Route 10, or Kessel Road. Follow the flow onto Kessel Rd. At some point, the name of the road changes to Route 10/6/AKA Morgantown-East Road. It's a total of 9.3 miles from the stoplight to the next stop sign at Patterson Creek Road. You will have ridden a fine stretch of road with hairpin turns, blind crests, and past the entrance to a working mine.

Turn left onto the double-yellow Patterson Creek Road. Follow the flow of this road left onto Route 42 and continue south 6.5 miles to Ridge Road. Turn right. Follow this high country lane 4.5 miles to a sharp, angular, downhill, left-hand turn onto Corners Road. Follow Corners Road 4.6 miles to a church, and then bear right to the main road, Route 28/55. Turn right.

Ride Rt. 28/55 for 1.7 miles. Keep your eyes peeled for Smoke Hole Road on the left. Turn left and stop at the bridge — and chill. That's right! Take a load off. Have a look around. You're looking at the longer North Branch of the Potomac River. (I've been to the source of the North Branch. It's where the river first bubbles up from out of the ground. It is marked by a boulder laid by surveyors in 1742, called the "Fairfax Stone.")

Check out the natural spring located just across the bridge on the right. Fill your water bottle with fresh spring water.

Smoke Hole Road is about as curvy and remote as it gets in West Virginia, and you are about to ride it. Fifteen years ago, Smoke Hole Rd. was entirely gravel. I rode it once on a BMW K75 RT touring bike. The first section was paved, and I was drawn into the vibe of the place. When the bike and I stepped down onto the gravel, I kept on plugging away, thinking my luck would turn. It didn't, and for another 11 miles or so, I was puckered tight, since the gravel was thickly laid and mushy with large stones. There's no way I'll ever take a chance riding alone like that again on a remote gravel road unless I know how long, and where the road is headed. I was exhausted afterward. You'll understand what I mean as you ride this stretch. Smoke Hole is now nicely paved with plenty of low-gear curves. It's very scenic as well, so take it easy. Have fun and enjoy the sights!

Roughly 12 miles later, you will cross a small bridge and arrive at a T-intersection. Turn left. Ride downhill about half a mile. Turn right. This is another scenic stretch through Smoke Hole Canyon along the South Branch of the Potomac River. (You'll get to its source tomorrow.) Ride 5.4 miles to the highway, Route 220. Turn right.

Ride 1.4 miles on Route 220. Beside a large white house on the left, turn left onto Schmucker Road. Ride 3 miles on Schmucker Road. Keep an eye peeled, and turn right onto Kiser Gap Road. Ride 2.9 miles and follow the flow of Kiser Gap Road to the right. Continue another 1.3 miles on Kiser Gap Road, turn right again, and follow it another 5.4 miles all the way to a T-intersection. Again this is another fine example of West Virginia back country invisible road motorcycling. Turn right onto Route 33.

Follow Rt. 33 for 2.5 miles into Franklin, West Virginia and the Shell gas station on the left. Stop and chill. This is a good opportunity to purchase gas.

After you're tanked up, continue north onto Route 220/33. Ride about half a mile, then turn left, and continue on Route 33. Follow Route 33 up and over Judy Gap. As you descend, keep an eye peeled for the overlook on the right. It's a view of the New Germany Valley, a beautiful West Virginia vista and worth a brief stop.

Afterward, continue roughly 14 miles to the stop sign at Seneca Rocks. The "rocks" at Seneca Rocks is a large limestone outcropping. When you consider that limestone is essentially a hardened slurry of piled crushed mollusk shells and sea coral, it's easy to conclude that Seneca Rocks is very, very old.

Seneca Rocks was also Paul Mihalka's favorite stop along one of his many journeys. I happened upon Paul here a couple of times while I was conducting Workshops since I had developed a fondness for the Park as well. He'd be sitting quietly at one of the shaded picnic tables and smile large as I rolled in. I'd smile back, very pleased with the coincidence. His license tag read OLDFRT.

Just before Paul died, he told his wife to ask me if I would carry his remains to Seneca Rocks for scattering. Of course I would, and of course I did - along with about 30 other riders I invited who loved Paul as well. His daughter Arianna even rode on the back of my motorcycle with me. Overall, we had quite a day. You will see I have routed you to a shady area off to the left of the Park. It's where Paul and I used to sit and talk.

Afterward, ride back to the stop sign and continue west on Route 33.

Ride approximately 12 miles and bear right onto Route 32. Continue 19.3 miles trending uphill onto the Cumberland Plateau, across Canaan Valley (3000 feet MSL) into, and just through the town of Davis, West Virginia. On the far side of town, I suggest you stay at the Alpine Inn on the right. The Alpine Inn is no beauty queen, but the beds are firm, the bathrooms are well lit, there's good shower pressure and the water's hot. Ask for Kathy. She owns it, and tell her I said "Hi." I've stayed there many nights. For dinner, I suggest you walk—that's right!—walk seven minutes back into town and dine at Sirianni's on the left. It's a bright and cheerful Italian cafe. You will be glad you did.

Total mileage for Day One: Approximately 236 miles. This may not seem like many miles for a full day of motorcycling. But you'll soon discover that with the curves, scenery, gas stops, and places of interest, it is enough.

Day Two: Davis, WV to Peaks of Otter Lodge, Bedford, VA

Before departing Davis, I suggest you eat breakfast at the Sawmill Restaurant since it is on the premises of the Alpine Inn. Gas up in Davis if you didn't the afternoon before. Then, turn north onto Route 32 and continue about 3 miles through the down-at-the-heel town of Thomas, West Virginia. Turn left onto Route 219, and prepare for an exciting 11.7-mile "sleigh ride" down the Plateau! Once at the bottom, turn left onto Route 72.

Route 72 is an iconic West Virginia byway. It's a small lane that's large on scenery. From where you turn, it stretches along the Cheat River. Take your time through here. The road can be a little gravely, and if you are out early, you're going to encounter local West Virginians on their way to work. Be careful, because their vehicles usually show up around blind corners! It's a great road, though, and I ride it every chance I get.

But you are not riding Route 72 to its conclusion! At roughly 13.6 miles, keep your eye peeled for Jenningston Road. Turn right.

This piece of road is invisible, all right. In 15 years, I have never seen another motorcycle through here, and rarely have I seen other traffic. Follow my instructions carefully. You are now headed into the folds of the Cumberland Plateau and the wilds of rural West Virginia - don't get lost! Follow this roughly-paved old road 2.2 miles downhill to a small bridge. Cross the Dry Fork River, and turn right onto Gladwin Road - there are great views through here! Use your imagination to picture an Indian hunting party camping along the river, because they did. Believe me, this is a remote and secluded area! Along the way, you will come upon an open field where there are several rusted-out travel-trailers parked alongside the river. Navigate carefully. Just beyond this area, at 3.1 miles from the last bridge, the road forks left onto Granville-Good Road. You'll then ride uphill into deep forest and onto dirt for a short bit. (Come to think of it, there's been logging activity here recently.) No worries. The road is well graded, and I've taken both Harley and Goldwing riders through here. Just don't run off the danged cliff, or you're a goner!

Soon the road returns to pavement. Bear to the right and enjoy following the flow of this macadam over hill and dale until you've ridden 4.1 miles. The flow of the road at this point will have you turning 90 degrees right onto Sully Road. Keep motoring, follow-following the flow 6.9 miles. You will finally pop out at an intersection with Route 33, the main road. There, you will see the Alpine Spring Restaurant on the right, a good place for coffee! (Note: from Rt. 72 and Jenningston Road to this restaurant is 16.5 miles.)

Now you have a choice: Paved or dirt. Either cross the main highway and continue straight through Glady and directly to Durbin, WV, 23 miles of which is on dirt. Or turn west onto Route 33 and follow the highway all the way around. Either way, you'll get to Durbin, an old railroad town.

If you chose dirt, ride straight across Route 33. You'll go 9.4 miles along a fine stretch of undulating, swooping, mountain road into the tiny isolated village of Gladys. There's not much there, so turn left and continue 0.3 miles. Turn right. Follow this road 23.4 miles, most all of which is decent dirt. You'll be paralleling the West Branch of the scenic Greenbrier River. It's remote wilderness through here, as if little has changed here in a thousand years. There will be lots of pretty scenery. You'll then enter the back streets of Durbin. Find your way to Route 250.

For those who prefer to stay on smooth pavement: Turn right onto Route 33 and motor 12 miles into downtown Elkins, West Virginia. There are pretty views along this stretch of Route 33. At the stoplight, turn left onto Route 219 and ride south nearly 18 miles. Turn left onto Route 250 and ride nearly 19 miles to Durbin.

Either way, from the Alpine Spring Restaurant, it is 32.4 slower miles of one, or 49.4 faster miles of another. Both ways get you to Durbin. Fuel is available in Durbin.

From Durbin, ride Route 250 east 20.5 miles out of West Virginia and into Virginia. This is also an outstanding stretch of smooth double-yellow, up and over several ridge lines and across various wilderness valleys. Beautiful scenery! It's fast and thrilling East Coast motorcycling, as great as anywhere!

Before long, you'll enter a beautiful region known as the Bluegrass Valley of Virginia. Keep your eyes peeled for a simple intersection in the middle of the Valley called Hightown. There are structures on either side at the corner that might block your view of the intersection. Turn left onto Route 640. Look around. It's gorgeous! Along the left, down in the low ground, you're going to see an assortment of valley streams. They'll converge to form the South Branch of the Potomac River. Follow the flow of Route 640 and the Potomac River through the Town of Bluegrass and beyond. Rt. 640 will become Rt. 642. Continue a total of 9.7 miles until you reach Route 220.

Turn right. Follow Route 220 for 6.5 miles into Monterey, VA. Turn right at the stoplight. There's gas and a good restaurant in Monterey called High's on the left, directly across from The Highland Inn.

I've stayed at the Inn several times in years past. It's an historic turn-of-the-last-century country hotel. When I stayed there years ago, the innkeeper told me an interesting story. Rumor has it that during the 1920s, German military cadets traveled to the area to study Thomas "Stonewall" Jackson's 1862 Shenandoah Campaign during the American Civil War. Evidently, the cadets were treated cordially, because a month or so after their return to Germany, the innkeeper received a handwritten letter from one of the cadets. The cadet was profuse in his appreciation for everything the innkeeper had done for them. The letter was signed - Erwin Rommel.

After lunch, follow Route 250 east about 10 miles to the small town of McDowell.

Turn right onto Route 678/AKA Indian Draft Road. Route 678 is one of the prettiest ribbons of asphalt in all of Virginia, and truly an invisible road. As you approach Williamsville, you'll ride through a shaded area. On the left is a short driveway to a parking area. You'll find a narrow footbridge there across the Cowpasture River to a secluded swimming hole.

Carefully follow Route 678. At 19.8 miles, Indian Draft Rd. will bend to the left, and cross the Cowpasture River.

Once, while staying with some friends who are fortunate to live in the area, and after a late summer swim, I was lounging along the banks of the Cowpasture River. I had dried off and was dozing in the warmth of late afternoon sunlight. I looked up and there, about 50 feet above the river, were thousands of butterflies bobbing and weaving along to places of mystery known only to them.

At 23.7 miles, Route 678 flows into Deerfield Rd. Bear right. Ride one mile. Turn right again onto Deerfield Road. Ride 6 miles. As you do, you'll cross a trout stream. Look to the left to see a nice fishing camp.

A strange thing happened to me a few years ago on this bridge. I was leading a Workshop, but we were riding in the opposite direction. We arrived on the bridge so suddenly, we caught a strange wild animal off guard. It was a dark black cat about the size and build of a bulldog. It had a bobbed tail, an unnaturally large head, a big face, and a wide mouth full of ferocious teeth. In an instant, six motorcycles were upon it as we crossed the bridge. The thing crouched against the cement side of the bridge as our wheels rolled by, bared its fangs and snarled at us. Then it was over. But I've always wondered what that animal was. A bobcat? But bobcats aren't black, so I just don't know.

Anyhow, soon you'll arrive at the stop sign of a major highway.

Turn left onto Route 39, another fine stretch of Virginia's best double-yellow two-lane highways. Follow

Route 39 east along the Maury River about 34 miles to Route 11 on the outskirts of Lexington, Virginia. Along the way, be sure to stop at the camera-ready overlook at Goshen Pass where the Maury cuts through a large canyon. You will also pass through Rockbridge Baths. In the 1870s, this was a popular spa catering to the elderly. After his retirement from military service, Robert E. Lee served as President of Washington University in Lexington. He used to take his wife, stricken with severe arthritis, by horse and buggy to the spa for relief.

There is also a fine collection of low-gear curves just as you approach the outskirts of Lexington.

There is much to see in Lexington. You could easily pass half a day or more here sightseeing. I particularly enjoy showing friends the "Recumbent Lee" sculpture of General Robert E. Lee in the Chapel of Washington and Lee University. The sculpture depicts the South's beloved General wearing battle dress, in repose on his battle cot, fast asleep. Positioned in the four corners surrounding the sculpture are Lee's original battle flagstaffs of the Army of Northern Virginia. Dignified indeed. Lee himself, along with members of his family, rest peacefully downstairs, along with Traveler, Lee's American Saddlebred war horse.

At the T-intersection, turn south onto Rt. 11 and ride through the commercial outskirts of Lexington. Follow Route 11 out of town and back into the Shenandoah countryside for about 15 miles. Follow the flow of the road onto Route 130 at Natural Bridge, VA toward Glasgow, VA.

Consider spending the night near Natural Bridge, a gigantic, granite spectacle of world class proportions and the centerpiece of Virginia's newest State Park. The view is definitely worth your time. Stop at the Visitor's Center and plan on being at the site for at least an hour. The Natural Bridge Hotel, though long-in-the-tooth, is adequate.

From Natural Bridge, ride Route 130 east about 15.5 miles to the fabulous Blue Ridge Parkway. As you ride Route 130, you will surely appreciate the fine set of swooping, on-camber curves you'll encounter along the James River. These lower-gear curves are a rider's delight and would hardly be discovered if a rider from elsewhere were on his own.

The Blue Ridge Parkway, or "BRP" as it's fondly called, is one of the most visited National Parks in the country. You would never know it, though. The Parkway, end-to-end, is 469 miles long, and it's rarely congested except during "leaf-peeper" season. I've ridden many tens of miles and never seen another car, and no trucks are allowed. But be careful — the speed limit is strictly enforced.

Once you reach the BRP, turn south and ride about 24 miles to Milepost 86 and the Peaks of Otter Lodge, one of two lodges in the Park.

This particular stretch of the Parkway is one of its prettiest and most dramatic. You'll cross the lowest part of the Parkway at the historic and peaceful James River. Then, over the next 20 miles, you'll make the climb to the highest point of the Parkway in Virginia at just over 4000 feet. It's a spectacular climb with large dramatic vistas and overlooks. I particularly like the Arnold Valley Overlook. This stretch is some of the prettiest motorcycling on the East Coast.

If you plan to stay at the Peaks of Otter Lodge, make reservations early because it books up fast. Double up if doable, because the rooms are spacious. Each room has a pleasant balcony overlooking Abbott Lake and Sharp Top Mountain. I am certain you'll enjoy your stay. You can either spend the night at the Lodge or camp at a nice nearby camping area. Either way, try to get there early if possible, or plan on spending two nights there.

There is much exploring to be done here on two feet as well as on two wheels. Peaks of Otter is bucolic and restful. At around 2500 feet, the Lodge is nestled between two mountains, Sharp Top and Flat Top, on the shore of Abbott Lake. The lake was named after Stanley Abbott, the Parkway's chief landscape architect. The view from the top of Sharp Top is splendid, with a 360-degree view of the surrounding area. To the east is Bedford, VA and the National D-Day Memorial. Proportionate to its size, Bedford lost more boys during the Second World War's Operation Overlord than did any other town or city in the country. There were 19 Gold Star mothers created that day (plus three more during the course of the Normandy Invasion). I like to think that each one of those beautiful boys had once climbed Sharp Top. You'll understand why they made the hike if you take the time to climb it as well.

Total mileage for Day Two: Approximately 253 miles.

Day Three: Peaks of Otter Lodge to Meadows of Dan, VA

Enjoy breakfast in the Lodge's rustic dinning room. Then saddle up and continue south 5.3 miles along the Parkway. There are some particularly sweet downhill curves through this short stretch.

Turn right onto Route 43 northbound and drop down off the Parkway toward Buchanan, Virginia. Rt. 43 is a steep drop-off so keep your gears low and your momentum in check. I suggest you gas up in Buchanan.

Turn north on Route 11 and ride 0.2 miles. Just across the James River, turn left onto Route 43, and motor cross-country about 14.5 miles through the small town of Eagle Rock. Continue on Route 43 a short distance out of town. Turn left and again cross the James River. Straight ahead, you'll see an impressive rock face. Turn right onto Route 220. Go about one mile and turn left onto Route 615/AKA Craig Creek Road. Ride 5.5 miles.

Before you turn right onto Route 621/AKA Roaring Run Road, you might stop and check out Craig Creek. Go ahead - stick your toes in. You are "far from the madding crowd" here. Savor this simple pleasure moment.

Afterward, wind gradually uphill about 4 miles on Roaring Run Rd. and follow the flow of the road bearing left onto Rich Patch Road. Continue another 3.8 miles. Keep your eyes peeled for Route 621/AKA Hayes Gap Road. Turn right. Ride Hayes Gap Rd. nearly 5 miles to Route 18. I get excited just detailing these roads to you. Truly, these are some of the most remote Appalachian roads you'll ever find, if find them you could!

Turn left onto Route 18 and enjoy another fine piece of asphalt. Rev up to a satisfying groove and roll for 19.6 miles, heading down to Paint Bank. At the stop sign, turn left, and soon you'll see the Swinging Bridge Restaurant and General Store on the right. Do stop and poke around. General stores like this are a real find.

From the General Store parking lot, turn right and ride south on Route 311. Run this super-smooth mountain pass about 11 miles and enjoy the high RPM, lower-gear switchbacks. Keep your eyes peeled for a large white house and cinderblock barn on the right. Turn a sharp downhill right onto Route 658.

What can I tell you but that Route 658 is yet another fantastic invisible road! Unless you know and appreciate the certain qualities of this road, you are just not going to turn onto it. I knew it was a "keeper" the first time I rode it. Ride 4.7 miles. Keep an eye peeled once again for Johns Creek Road, AKA/Route 632. Turn left. Ride 9.6 miles. You'll reconnect to Route 658 at a crossroad called Maggie. And again, take your time to look around!

Bear right, then left. Follow Route 632/658 0.8 miles. Turn left again on Rt. 658 and ride south 4.2 miles to Route 42, sometimes called the Shenandoah Parkway. Turn right. Ride exactly 8.8 miles. If you arrive in Newport, you've ridden too far.

Turn right onto Route 601 (Clover Hollow Road). Follow the flow of this road along quiet Sinking Creek which, around a sharp left curve, turns into Route 604/AKA Zells Mill Road. You'll pass a restored wooden covered bridge. Continue a total of 2.1 miles on this short but nice stretch of macadam until you reach Route 700/AKA Mountain Lake Road.

Turn right and rumble uphill 6.3 miles to Mountain Lake. There, you'll reach the small Mountain Lake Lodge Resort. Just don't look for the lake. It was drained several years ago by a small local earthquake. The fieldstone lodge was used as the backdrop in the 1987 Patrick Swayze/Jennifer Grey film "Dirty Dancing." Stop here for lunch. Afterward, turn back down the mountain. Go 100 yards or so

The Art of Riding Smooth

and turn right onto Doe Creek Road. Spin back down the mountain about 5 miles to what will be a major four-lane highway, Route 460. Turn left. Ride 2.8 miles to Route 730. Turn right.

Continue on Route 730 for 11.5 miles. You'll cross the New River. More on this river a little later. You will finally arrive at a four-lane highway, Route 100. Turn left and ride 4.6 miles. Turn right onto Little Creek Rd. It is a little road, too, so watch for it. Ride 12 miles. Little Creek is yet again just a neat, zippy ribbon of valley road burrowed between two long ridge lines.

Turn left onto Robinson Tract Road (Route 738). Robinson Tract Rd. is a tight, technical, and sometimes sandy series of switchbacks over a fairly high ridge. Be careful. Stay tight to the right around both left and right switchbacks and stay on your game. Every year, there's at least one motorcycle crash through here. Ride 9.7 miles. You're going to enter the back street outskirts of Pulaski, Virginia, a small manufacturing city in SW Virginia that's seen better days.

What you'll do now is ride through one of the more pleasant neighborhoods of Pulaski. Turn left onto 16th Street NE. Ride a block and turn right onto Prospect Avenue. Ride 0.9 mile. At the T-intersection, turn left on Route 11. Ride 0.1 mile and turn right on Edgehill Drive. Ride 0.3 miles out to Route 99, another highway. Turn left.

Ride 3.2 miles, crossing over Interstate 81, to the T-intersection. Turn left. Ride 0.4 miles. Turn right onto Lowman's Ferry Road and ride 3.6 miles across Claytor Lake. I always stop at the convenience store on the right just before crossing the lake. It's my final stop before making the final push back to the top of the Blue Ridge Mountains.

At the T-intersection, turn left onto Lead Mine Road. You'll then motor 9.3 miles back along the northern base of the Blue Ridge itself. At some point, you will cross the Little River which was once a convenient thoroughfare for early settlers and Native People. Keep your eye peeled for Indian Valley Road and get prepared for one of the finest Blue Ridge Mountain roads in all of SW Virginia!

Turn right. Follow Indian Valley Rd. You will be heading south and trending uphill 13.1 miles. You'll get to where Indian Valley Road forks and continues both ways. Follow the left fork and continue another 5.7 miles to the T-intersection at Route 221. Turn left.

Ride 0.7 miles and bear right onto Route 799/AKA Conner-Grove Road. Follow the road 8.8 miles, climbing and twisting up this fine piece of the road until you once again reach the Blue Ridge Parkway, running along what's known as the Blue Ridge Plateau.

Turn right. Ride less than 0.2 miles and turn left onto a small nondescript road. Ride up the road about

200 yards and behold: The Woodberry Inn! You'll spend your third night here.)Note: Plan ahead to ensure the dining room is open.)

Total mileage for Day Three: Approximately 204 miles.

Day Four: Meadows of Dan, VA to the Pisgah Inn, NC

You can either enjoy the complimentary breakfast at the Woodberry or, even better, just have coffee at the Woodberry. You can then ride down the Parkway a short piece and order a legit farm-fresh breakfast at the Poor Farmer's Market in Meadows of Dan. To do so, go back to the Parkway and turn south. Ride 3.6 miles and exit toward Stuart. Come off the ramp and turn east on Old Route 58. Poor Farmer's Market is part of a Marathon gas station on the right. Walk right in and order yourself a big ol' country breakfast from one of the pretty local mountain girls working the deli. You might even meet Felecia, the owner. She has been my hillbilly friend for nearly 20 years through good times and bad. I half-jokingly call her the "Queen" of Meadows of Dan. Felecia has never had a danged thing handed to her. "Been dirt poor" she's proud to say. She used her knowledge of locally- grown produce passed down from her grandmother, her God-given talent and mountain gumption to build a business that's one of the most popular establishments along the Parkway. Take a good look around the store. She'll be the one with radiant, watchful blue eyes, and if you happen to spot her, give her my compliments!

The Poor Farmer's Market is where the local mountain people come to buy produce, share business opportunities, get the scoop on local gossip, swap stories, and praise the great weather. Motorcyclists have also congregated there for years. In a word, the Market is authentic.

After breakfast, I suggest you take a brief detour and visit Willville, a T.W.O. That's right! It's one of several "Two Wheels Only" motorcycle camp-grounds throughout the mountains. In fact, if you prefer to camp instead of staying at the Woodberry Inn, this is the perfect place for you!

Turn left out of the Poor Farmer's Market and ride straight and slightly downhill about one mile. Just beyond a rise, you'll see the Willville Bike Camp sign on the left. I've camped, slept in the private cabin, or bunked in the bunkhouse many times. Owner Will Beers built Willville out of an impenetrably thick rhododendron forest.

There's a good story here. Will's a "Connecticut Yankee" from Danbury. He lived down the mountain about two hours away in Winston-Salem, North Carolina. Over the years, he developed a hankering to create a motorcycle campground. After many months of searching, he finally landed these 25 acres on the Plateau. He then spent the next several years coming up the mountain on his days off with his chainsaw and a gas can, clearing the ungodly thick flora and fauna growing deep in the forest. Exhausted, he usually found himself after each day's work slumped on one of the many rocking chairs on the meeting porch of the Poor Farmer's Market, working on an ice cream cone. After many months, local folks became curious about what this exhausted city slicker who kept returning to the market, dirty and all beat up, was up to.

It wasn't long before a much-respected mountain of a man named Buford sat down next to Will and straight-up asked him. Will told Buford his story. Buford sat there slowly scratching his chin and listening intently. After moments of quiet, Buford turned to Will and made him a simple offer. He suggested to Will that they meet up at Will's property the following weekend. Will arrived early. Then, right on time, up over the rise came Buford in a tractor-trailer with his bulldozer loaded on back! Together, they were able to finish clearing the land that weekend, something that would have taken Will several more years to accomplish alone. All the debris was then piled a mile high in the middle of the clearing and set afire. The ashes from that huge bonfire created the foundation for the field that is now enjoyed by so many motorcyclists who come to camp at Willville. Sadly, Buford died a few years ago. His great big heart tuckered and finally gave out.

Anyhow, Will is a generous and kind soul. He's also a master guide and, when prompted, rides like the wind. Will's a man worth getting to know, as is his ace riding buddy, Mike Shepherd. Mike's a 70-something former West Virginia coal truck driver who also knows his roads. Whenever I catch a "flight" with these two flyboys, it's great fun, and they bring my game up as well! I owe a lot to both of these characters for generously showing me around the area.

When you are finished visiting, turn right out of Willville and continue back on through Meadows of Dan until you reach Route 58, the main highway. Turn right toward Stuart. You are now going to ride downhill and off the Blue Ridge Plateau.

Ride exactly 12.9 miles. Just after another Marathon gas station on the right, exit to the right off the main road onto Route 58-Bus. Follow the flow of the road through a stop sign or two and at least one stoplight 1.2 miles. Turn right onto Main Street. If you feel like it, there's a good coffee shop a block down on the left.

Continue downhill 0.2 miles following the flow of Main St. and bear right onto Dobbins Road. Follow the flow of Dobyns Road where, at some point, it will flow onto Little Dan River Road. You will now be riding along the southern base of the Blue Ridge Plateau. You'll see the cliffside a few miles off to the right. Ride 13.4 miles winding along a nice lane-and-a-half country road with little traffic. In fact, you will have probably already noticed the utter dearth of traffic along the entire route!

At the stop sign, turn a sharp right onto Route 103. Ride 0.6 miles and turn right onto Route 733/AKA Ararat Road. Ride 4.6 miles. Turn right again onto Squirrel Spur Road and motor uphill 7.1 miles back to the Blue Ridge Parkway. That's right! We could have ridden straight down the Parkway, but we didn't. We detoured solely for the love of the ride! Squirrel Spur, uphill, is an especially enjoyable, smoothly paved stretch of road. I couldn't have you on the Blue Ridge Plateau without having you ride it.

Continue 30.6 miles south along the fabulous Blue Ridge Parkway. I've ridden this lovely ridge line ribbon many times. In addition to my Blue Butt 1000, I've ridden the entire Parkway top-to-bottom and bottom-to-top nonstop several times over the course of a single day. Either way it is a curve-carving drill that I never get tired of, plus there's no navigation needed! Exit off the Parkway just south of the North Carolina line onto Route 18 toward Sparta.

Turn right and ride 1.6 miles. Turn left onto Glade Valley Road. This is a fine stretch of rolling North Carolina high country. You'll see large Christmas tree farms with their small evergreens forming large geometric patterns across the hillsides. There are also several large, fragrant boxwood farms with thousands of plants beautifully displayed. Far off over yonder at about "one o'clock," you'll see Mount Rogers, the tallest mountain in Virginia at 5,728 feet. That's where we're headed.

The Magical Mountainous Tour

Follow the flow of Glade Valley Rd. about 11.7 miles. Turn right onto Route 21. Soon you'll be passing through Sparta, North Carolina. There are a few restaurants and gas stations here. Continue a total of 7.7 miles on Rt. 21. Then bear left on Route 221, ride 0.9 mile and turn right onto Route 93.

Route 93 is a favorite rolling ribbon of mine. Its bright double-yellow over jet-black asphalt beckons me. It's a glorious higher-gear, high-speed, overland groove. Ride 10.8 miles to the T-intersection just past a bridge across the New River.

The New River is very interesting. It was discovered in 1654 by a local explorer, Abraham Wood, who happened on it. He tried to name the river after himself, but as more explorers discovered for themselves this "new" river, the description stuck - hence the New River. Geologists, however, differ. The river is not new! In fact, they say the river is likely the oldest river in the world! We know the Appalachians are old, but the river is even older. Its headspring does not spring from these mountains. Instead, the river passes through the mountains. This means the river was there before the mountains existed!

From its source to its mouth on the Ohio River at Point Pleasant, WV (some 360 miles downstream) the river served as a major paddle-way for Native People as they traded and hunted in these wild mountains.

Turn left onto Route 58 and ride alongside the river through Mouth of Wilson. Then continue on Route 16/58 a total of 5.5 miles to Volney. Turn left onto Rt. 58. At the intersection, there's a decent country restaurant for a cup of coffee and a bio-break. Then continue west on Route 58 toward Damascus.

Route 58/AKA J.E.B. Stuart Highway is a great road. Several years ago, I had an article published about my experiences in and around this highway. I nominated it the finest piece of Virginia asphalt as can be found in this most beautiful Mid-Atlantic State. Ride Rt. 58 along the slope of Mt. Rogers 11.2 miles. Turn left onto Route 751/AKA Sturgill Road. (We'll catch the entire stretch of Rt. 58 on our return trip.)

Ride 3.5 miles. Turn or bear right onto Route 194 and continue 8.4 miles to Warrensville. Turn right onto Route 88 and continue another 21 miles. Again, there is no way a rider from elsewhere is going to choose these roads to ride. It's a twisty middle-gear groove with plenty of middle- and lower-gear curves. Lovely! As you cross state lines into Tennessee, the road changes to Route 67. Ride Rt. 67 for 1.6 miles to the main highway. Turn left onto Route 421. Follow Rt. 421 along 8.3 miles back into North Carolina, and turn right back onto Route 194.

Before you do, you might check out the Mast General Store in Vilas, North Carolina. It's a well-equipped store with all manner of interesting products, from a wide selection of fishing gear and clothing to barrels of candy, many of which haven't been widely distributed since the 1960s. Clark Bar anyone?

Turn south onto Route 194. This stretch is twisty-twisty with many low-gear curves, up and over several steep hills, all on great pavement. After about 12 miles you'll come into Banner Elk, elevation 3700 feet. Banner Elk is a well-heeled resort town west of Boone, North Carolina. Along the ridge lines, you'll see many expensive vacation homes. Banner Elk even has its own private airport for local fat cats' traveling convenience. Continue through Banner Elk on Rt. 194 another 6.9 miles, and turn right onto Route 19E.

You'll see signs for Elk Park Falls. If you have the time, the waterfall is an impressive sight. It's 45 feet high and from its sheer volume alone, worth a look. If not, continue west northwest on Rt. 19E back into Tennessee. Turn left onto Route 143 toward Roan Mountain State Park.

This next section is a most excellent stretch of motorcycling. It just doesn't get much better. Continue through the verdant State Park and you'll start climbing, eventually to over a mile high. I always stop at the Roan Mountain summit in the bright fresh air. You'll see hikers and other folks like you who love being out-of-doors.

As you twist down off the mountain, you'll re-enter North Carolina. The route number changes to Route 261. From Route 19E, ride a total of 24.5 miles. Keep your eye peeled for Cub Creek Road. Turn right. Cub Creek is a 1.5-mile twisty shortcut that will get you over to Route 226. Turn right. Ride 0.5 mile and turn left onto Route 80. Follow Rt. 80 for 2.6 miles. Turn right and continue on Rt. 80.

If Rt. 80 were a snow ski run, it would be marked "black diamond." It's a 10.6-mile long expert stretch with good pavement, but it's twisty-twisty, so be careful-careful. At the main highway, turn to the right and back onto Route 19E. Follow it 1.4 miles. Turn left and follow Rt. 80 almost 14 miles up the mountain and all the way to the Blue Ridge Parkway.

The Blue Ridge Parkway reminds me of Maurice Ravel's masterpiece, "Bolero." https://www.youtube.com/watch?v=dZDiaRZy0Ak. The song goes on for about 17 minutes. The last few minutes end in a towering crescendo with drums and cymbals clashing. The Parkway also ends in a crescendo with high altitudes, smoky fog, large cliffs, big panoramic scenery, blowing wind and the freshest air.

From Rt. 80 and the Parkway, continue roughly 64 miles south to Milepost 408/408 and the Pisgah Inn, the second of two lodges on the Blue Ridge Parkway. For those who like to camp, there's a very nice campground across the Parkway from the Inn. I've camped there and can vouch for it; it even has hot showers! Either way, have a good night! You've earned it!

Total mileage for Day Four: Approximately 241 miles.

Day Five: Two Choices

You are now along the crest of the Blue Ridge Parkway and within a day's striking distance of some of the best technical motorcycling found anywhere in the world. There are so many terrific options to consider! Certainly "The Dragon" at Deal's Gap and the Cherohala Skyway are major considerations; both are extraordinary. Many riders feel that Deal's Gap has become over-publicized and on perfect spring, summer, and fall weekends, the venue is definitely crowded. But if you can plan on getting there during the middle of the week, the congestion isn't bad. The gap is twisty, for sure: 318 lower-gear curves in 11 miles! There isn't a road with more coils, twists, and turns anywhere in the United States!

The Cherohala Skyway is roughly 35 miles long, with plenty of middle-gear curves. Each overlook is amazing as well. Whenever I ride either Deal's Gap and/or the Cherohala Skyway, I ride them both directions. These roads are so good they deserve to be ridden twice!

While these two roads are special, I would say that relative to the all curvy road riding you've already done, both roads may feel slightly anti-climactic. Plus, it will take a lot of "getting" to get there, since both the Cherohala and Deal's Gap are on the far side of the mountains. Remember, these roads will always be there.

Instead, allow me to suggest two days of great lesser-known roads throughout the greater Asheville Area. These two routes were shared with me by two local experts, each of whom has made it a point to know his roads.

Greater Asheville Southern Route

This Southerly Route was shared with me by Wayne Busch. Wayne is the creator of http:// americaridesmaps.com.

After breakfast, continue south on the BRP. Ride 3.6 miles, and exit north onto Route 276 toward Curso or Canton. Be careful—the road is steep, deeply shaded, and can be slippery. At 6.1 miles, I suggest you stop at the Blue Ridge Motorcycle Campground on the right. This is another T.W.O. campground and a cool place to check out. Just don't stay long. You've got some serious mountain riding to do! Out of the campground, turn right and continue 8.4 miles to the stoplight in Curso. Turn left onto Route 215. Rt. 215 is ultimately an uphill grade back to the Parkway. But you'll ride along a valley road first, then cross alongside a placid mountain lake. There will be a tight right-hander by a roaring mountain cataract as you once again make the climb back to the crest of the Blue Ridge. As you crest, continue south on Route 215/AKA Parkway Road.

Rt. 215 becomes a steep downhill grade of super-smooth pavement. Steeply undulating roads can be a challenge, especially with a disrespectful attitude toward them. I'm reminded of another rider in my Workshop several years ago. From Upstate New York, he rode a gorgeous black BMW K1200LT Custom. It was one of the late-model heavy touring jobs with the power center-stand. I called his mount "Black Beauty." As we rode the rolling hills of the Maryland Piedmont, the fella handled his bike well, riding with nice lines. Once we got closer to the base of the Blue Ridge Parkway, I gathered the riders around me and cautioned them to use their lower gears when we began to make the climb. At one point, I heard him say his "go-to" gear was fourth gear. He called it his "all-in-one" gear. I replied that maybe in his neighborhood, fourth gear is a great all around gear - but NOT here in these mountains. I especially emphasized the importance of second gear since it gives a rider effective engine braking over relatively long distances. Soon we were making the climb up Route 56, through Montebello, along the Tye River. I was number two in our formation, concentrating on a rider ahead of me who was leading with Mr. Black Beauty behind me. Anyway, around a certain left hand curve, the road plummets steeply. It's easy to gain instant momentum. Being in a lower gear and rolling off the throttle instantly checks that momentum and keeps a bike under control. As I went around this curve, I felt tension in my gut and immediately looked in my rear view mirror only to see Mr. Black Beauty disappear in a cloud of dust into some bushes.

I braked hard and, once stopped, kept the transmission in gear so on a downhill slope, the bike would not roll off the side-stand. I chugged 25 yards up the hill, helmet on, and into the bushes where I knew this fella and his once-spotless black touring bike would be. He was there, full of adrenaline and trying like mad to lift his bike himself. I got in there along with another rider, and together we were able to lift the bike and push it back out onto the pavement. Oh boy, was I curious — I switched his ignition on and looked at his gear indicator display. Sure enough — fourth gear! I chose not to rub the fact in, and later Mr. Black Beauty came to tell me rather sheepishly that he most definitely had learned his lesson.

From the top of the Parkway, ride downhill 10.9 miles. Turn right onto Macedonia Church Road. Follow the flow of Macedonia Church Road onto Kitchen Loop Road. After 5.2 miles, you will arrive at the T-intersection. Turn right onto Silversteen Road. Ride 4 miles. Silversteen Rd. will flow onto Route 281/AKA Canada Road. Oh boy, what a dynamite road! This is the kind of road that East Coast "curve junkies" dream about. There are several segments that lace together 10 or 12 consecutive S-curves up and over some big hills. Mighty fine! These curves are so good we're going to ride them on the rebound! Continue 17.2 miles on Rt. 281 to the T-intersection. There's a convenience store on the right if a bio's necessary (since there's no such thing as a too empty bladder, eh?)

Turn right onto Route 107. Continue 5.5 miles to a stoplight. Turn left onto Cullowhee Mountain Road. Ride one mile. The road will fork. Follow the flow to the right onto Tilley Creek Road which will then flow into Ellijay Road. Follow Ellijay Road as it twists and turns down a grade 16 miles long through shady forests and splashing brooks until Ellijay Road finally spills out onto Route 64.

Turn left. Follow Rt. 64 for 2.9 miles. Turn left again onto Walnut Creek Road and ride back up the grade. Walnut Creek Rd. will flow into Pine Creek Road. Keep on going until you ride 8.9 miles. Turn right onto North Norton Road.

Follow North Norton Rd. 1.9 miles. Then bear to your right on Yellow Mountain Road. Ride downhill about 6 miles. Turn left onto Norton Road and follow back it back to North Norton Road. Turn right. Follow North Norton Road until it intersects with Route 107. Turn right and follow it into the affluent resort town of Cashiers, North Carolina. There are a number of nice restaurants in Cashiers. Find one to your liking, and enjoy what will likely be a delicious lunch.

Afterward, continue south onto Route 107. Ride 1.8 miles through expensive neighborhoods and turn right again onto Whiteside Cove Road, with more high-end vacation neighborhoods on either side. Ride 7.5 miles. Great pavement. Tight turns. Whiteside Cove Rd. will flow right onto Horse Cove Road. Follow it. Again, great pavement and very, very twisty-twisty! Follow Horse Cove Rd. into Highlands, North Carolina which is another high-end resort town. Check out Highlands if you'd like. Nice shops! Coffee. Clothing. Jewelry. Golf. Tennis. T-shirts and ice cream. It's all there.

Turn right back onto Route 64. Ride out of town 6.4 miles to Norton Road. Turn left and head back up the mountain. You are now going to backtrack Norton Rd. You'll ride by Yellow Mountain Road. This stretch should be slightly familiar since you are backtracking. At the intersection, turn sharp left instead of right and continue on North Norton Road 1.9 miles to Pine Creek Road. Now continue straight onto Pine Creek Rd. Ride nearly one mile. Turn left onto Cullowhee Mountain Road. This is a twisty little number that's going to take you nearly 10 miles over hill and dale back to Route 107. Turn right and ride the 5.5 miles back to Route 281. Turn left and make your way back 14.3 miles.

You're going to cross back over a reservoir. You'll then ride another half-mile or so. Keep your eye peeled for Wolf Mountain Road. Bear left. Ride one mile. Turn right and continue 7.5 miles on Tanasee Creek Rd. Turn left on Parkway Rd and motor back up the Parkway, continuing back to the Pisgah Inn.

Total miles for Day Five, the Southern Route: Approximately 204. Thank you, Wayne.

Day Six: Greater Asheville Northern Route

This Northerly Route that I am about to describe was shown to me by my friend, Ed Irwin. Ed's a local Greater Asheville rider whom I met several years ago while attending my booth at a BMW rally in Asheville. He told me that everybody who said they had taken my course told him they really learned a lot of neat stuff they didn't know. He asked if he could be of any assistance. I asked him whether he knew any cool roads around the Greater Asheville area. His eyes lit up and in an unhurried drawl, he commented that Asheville was his home town, and he'd been riding the region for over 40 years. "So yeah, I know some pretty cool roads, all right." With that, I eagerly brightened. We shook hands and agreed to get together immediately after the rally and ultimately wound up spending two full days on the road together. I've since returned to Asheville a couple of times alone and with friends to hook up with him and do further riding. Yeah, Ed knows some pretty cool roads, all right!

After breakfast, continue south on the BRP. Ride 3.6 miles and exit north onto Route 276 and once again ride to the stoplight in Curso. On the far corner is the Juke Box Restaurant, not a bad place for breakfast. Turn right and follow Route 215/AKA Pisgah Drive 13.8 miles. You are now in the paper mill town of Canton, North Carolina. Maybe you can smell pulp smoke! Turn right on Main Street. Go 0.3 miles and fork left onto Bridge Street. Go just a short distance and turn right onto Newfound Street. Ride 1.4 miles and turn left onto Beaverdam Road.

Follow the flow of Beaverdam Rd. 7.7 miles up and over a large ridge. Be careful on the back slope that you don't gather too much momentum. It's steep and twisty on the way down. There are several steep turns where you will benefit from using your rear brake as you enter and ride on through. At some point, Beaverdam Rd. flows into Willow Creek Road. Just follow the flow.

At the T-intersection, turn right and continue 2.3 miles. Turn right onto Sandy Mush Road. Follow the road 2.4 miles. Watch carefully for a left turn across a bridge, because from around a curve, it comes on suddenly. Turn left and continue on Sandy Mush Creek Road 2.4 miles to Route 63. At the stop sign, turn left and follow Rt. 63 for 11.7 miles up and over a large ridge line, and continue to the stop sign beside a left-side convenience store.

Turn right onto North Carolina Route 209, otherwise referred to as "The Rattler." It's a great stretch of road that will take you 14.6 miles into the little river town of Hot Springs, North Carolina situated along the French Broad River. Great place with cool people who have chosen to live there.

Follow the flow of the road onto Route 25 across the river and follow it 5.1 miles down a long sweeping grade to a T-intersection. There is a hippie coffee stand on the right. Turn right and spin your way up the hill. Great curves! Ride 2.0 miles. Turn left onto Lonesome Mountain Road, a very technical "Black Diamond." The road surface can be sandy at times, so by all means, stay on your game! Ride 3.6 miles. You'll arrive at Revere Road.

When Ed Irwin and I arrived at Revere Road, we pulled alongside one another. Ed lifted his face shield, turned to me and said with a smile, "You know Jim, when all you "interlopers" congregate at Deal's Gap stinking it up for us locals, we ride over here to Revere. May I present to you our "Deal's Gap." We call it 'Severe Revere'!" With that, he happily waved me through for my first crack at this most excellent remote, rural, not-too-refined, twisty as hell, invisible road.

Turn sharp right. Then ride this "bronco" 6.1 miles. Careful now! I've seen riders go wide. You'll end up at Big Laurel Road. Take a breath and merge to the right onto Big Laurel and continue winding along a pretty stream another 11.6 miles. You'll wind up just underneath Interstate 26 at a T-intersection. Look to your right. You'll see a small local diner, the Little Creek Cafe. Nice folks in there. Go for coffee and a tasty slice of homemade pie.

Turn left onto Route 23 and motor 8.8 miles. You'll arrive at Tilson Mountain Road.

Turn right, and ride around a large field with a farmhouse along the right side. Continue on Tilson

Mountain Rd., and you'll disappear into a forest where Tilson then becomes like an old goat trail.

Follow the road 4.4 miles. Turn hard right onto Route 19W and follow it 11.8 miles up and over some steep grades along a splashing creek. You'll arrive at a bridge crossing at 19W and Hunting Dale Road. Stop and savor the remoteness.

When you're finished, turn around and ride all the way back to Route 23! That's right! Great roads have to be ridden both ways, and after this gem, I think you'll agree.

On your return, when you are just getting out of the forest and see that initial big field ahead of you, you have the option of turning hard right onto a direct shortcut to Route 23. Go straight. Don't take the shortcut! The turn is treacherous. I know! It's where I once tipped over!!

Once you're back on Route 23, ride 1.3 miles. Make a sharp left turn onto Route 352. The route will change numbers to Route 212 as you again cross state lines. Ride 352/212 for 18.3 miles until you reach Route 208. Turn left. Ride 3.5 miles. Turn right onto Route 25 and ride the 5.1 miles back and uphill into Hot Springs. There are good restaurants in Hot Springs. My favorite is the Iron Horse Station Restaurant and Tavern on the left, just over and then along the railroad tracks.

After lunch, we're going to expedite getting back to the Pisgah Inn. Tomorrow will be a long day. So get back on "The Rattler" (Rt. 209) and take it 32.8 miles to Interstate 40. Take I-40E 10.6 miles and take the exit 31 ramp at Canton. Turn right and follow Route 215 back to Route 276. Turn left at the light. Follow Rt. 276 back to the Parkway. Turn north and return to the Pisgah Inn.

Total miles for the northern route, Day Six: approximately 234. Thanks, Ed!

Day Seven: Pisgah Inn NC to Floyd, VA

Today we will begin our return northward. The key to this day is getting an early start. Don't dawdle and leave at 10. You want to be under way at your earliest opportunity before rush hour in Asheville, as well as to get a jump on what will be a full day of motorcycling. We're going to expedite across Greater Asheville to get us more quickly back on the good stuff.

Turn north out of the Pisgah Inn and ride 2.8 miles. Turn left onto Route 151 and ride it nearly 12 miles down the mountain, across some straights to the stoplight. Turn right onto Route 23 and ride several miles to Interstate 40. Get on I-40E and ride east. Exit onto I-240N. Follow I-240N to Route 19. Follow Rt. 19 onto Route 25. Ride this combination of roads roughly 25 miles and exit onto Route 197 at Jupiter and turn right toward Barnardsville.

Route 197 is an interesting stretch of road. Ride through Barnardsville. You'll ride a total of about 10 miles. Then - surprise! The road turns to gravel and is a must-ride because it's a significant shortcut. The surface is well graded and usually void of significant traffic. It's dense forest here. I often stop, take off my helmet and remove my earplugs. I never feel that I've arrived anywhere until I stand once again on terra firma and remove my earplugs. Adding my sense of hearing in a new environment grounds me to wherever I've stopped. This is a deeply forested, tranquil place. Just listen...

On the backside of this stretch, you're going to come down an interesting set of multiple switchbacks on nice pavement. When you look back up the steep slope from where you've come, you'll have earned an interesting view, and the satisfaction that you've made it through safely. You'll continue on Rt. 197 for another 21 miles until you get to the main highway, Route 19. Turn left.

Ride 3.5 miles and turn right onto Jacks Creek Road, another rural gem. Follow the flow of Jacks Creek Road up the grade about 10 miles. Turn right onto Green Mountain Road.

Follow Green Mountain Road 1.5 miles and turn left back onto Route 197. Turn left again and ride 4.5 miles. At the intersection, there's a convenience store on the left. It's a nice place for a break. Then turn left and soon bear to the left continuing on Rt. 197 another 2.1 miles. Turn right onto Harrell Hill Road. Keep bearing to the right and follow Harrell Hill 3.1 miles until you reach Route 226. Turn right onto Route 226 and follow it 5 miles. What you've done is made a big loop, for no other reason, again, than for the love of the ride.

Turn left back onto Cub Creek Road. Follow Cub Creek Road back to Route 261 and retrace Route 261/143 back up and over the mountain and ride the 24.2 miles all the way back to Route 19E.

Turn right and continue retracing. Ride back to Route 194 and turn left. Take Rt. 194 back to Vilas. Maybe stop in Vilas again for a light snack.

All that was backtracking. Now, in just a bit, things are going to get super interesting. Follow Route 421 all the way through the far side of Mountain City, Tennessee. It's a bit of a haul at 47.4 miles but it's a fast road over interesting, mountainous terrain. So lay a spur into that motorcycle of yours, and get on down the road!

Once you're on the far side of Mountain City, get ready for another East Coast iconic twisty. Behold: "The Snake"!/AKA Route 421 out of Mountain City and into Shady Grove, TN. The length of "The Snake" is about 7.1 miles. It's a second gear screamin' corkscrew, so have fun! Afterward, stop at the Country Store at Shady Valley. The store features a wall and ceiling of shame, decorated with broken motorcycle parts from riders who weren't as careful as you've been. If you get there on a nice day, there could be a 100 motorcycles from all over the South. Shady Valley is definitely a destination crossroads for motorcycle riders from all around.

Once you have checked things out, saddle up, and turn north on Route 133 for the 13.3 mile run into Damascus. I have always liked Route 133, which turns into Route 91 when you cross the state line back into Virginia. The road is smooth with some super middle-gear, high-speed sweepers on the way through.

There are also a couple of landmarks to check out just south of Damascus. One is obvious; the other not so much. The first is Backbone Tunnel, built in 1901, and the shortest tunnel in the U.S. That's right! It's only 20 feet long! Close by is a Virginia Parks and Recreation outdoor pavilion set back from the road. Check it out. I've got a nice story about it to share.

Many, many years ago I was riding through here and pulled into the pavilion parking area. I had been riding hard, wanting to experience "The Snake" and then get back to Meadows of Dan all in one day, but I didn't take my own advice and left late. It was hot, and the cool, grassy shade of the park beckoned me. I took my water bottle and walked over to sit outside the pavilion under the boughs of a large oak tree. Minutes ticked by as I rested, contemplating how far I had been that day in literal as well as figurative ways: I was a far geographical distance from home, certainly, but also culturally. The people I had met were such a far cry from those I knew around Greater Washington, DC. Being in the moment, I also recognized I that had come a long way spiritually as well. Motorcycling had indeed provided me with just the kind of adventurous life I had yearned for. How else would I ever have experienced these great mountains the way I had, or found myself in such a faraway place as this, and met all the great people who had come across my path? I felt blessed and a profound sense of gratitude washed over me. I thanked "the powers that be" and was very peaceful.

Right about then, a beat-up old pickup truck chugged into view and rattled into the parking area. The motor gave a sigh as the driver shut the thing down. As he got out, the driver looked over at the motorcycle appreciatively and glanced at the odometer. I believe it read about 120,000 miles. He then reached into the bed of his truck and pulled out two white plastic garbage bags. I could tell they were full — but of what? The man was elderly and hillbilly in appearance but not in any derogatory way. He was just "country." Slowly, he walked out into the warm, sun-dappled lawn next to the pavilion and over to an old stump. There, he poured the contents of both bags around it. The contents was garbage — kitchen vegetable waste, banana skins, old onions and the like - all biodegradable stuff.

Then he ambled over my way, and as he did, he glanced at his watch and mumbled, "...about fifteen minutes." Then he drawled, "Nice bike. Looks like you've been doin' some ridin'. " He asked if I had been inside the pavilion. I told him I hadn't. He asked me if

I'd like to see it. I said, "Sure." We walked in together, and this old mountain man then proceeded to tell me all about how, back in '36, the pavilion was built.

It was built by local young men—all members of the then Civilian Conservation Corps. His father was the crew's foreman, and this old fella was proud of his father's work. The entire structure was built by hand. In those days, there were no gas-powered hand tools and certainly no electrical outlets. The massive American Chestnut support beams holding up the slate tile roof were of whole, bark-on, tree trunks and hand-hewn, as were the many thick wooden crossbeams. Trees like that don't even exist anymore! Iron screws, some over eight feet long, were plumbed true and hand-bolted into one log and then down into another and yet another. Each log and every hole was aligned perfectly. My impromptu guide went on to explain how the floor was laid with large, super-heavy granite boulders, all rolled into place, then mortared together with homemade cement and finally smoothed. The hand-built fire hearth was beautiful, with each stone placed carefully. I had no idea! This guy was fascinating and brought the fruition of his dad's pavilion to life. His articulation and gestures sparkled with intelligence and obvious appreciation for the hard labor done so well so long ago.

Pretty soon he started looking at his watch, and soon after, I heard a flock (a murder, actually) of crows congregating and cawing outside. "Yup." He chuckled. "They're right on time." It didn't take long for that "murderous" group of big black birds to make short work of the garbage scattered about. In about seven or eight minutes, the stump was picked clean, and the birds scattered to the four winds. As their caws faded into the distance, all that remained were leaves ruffling in the quiet. We introduced ourselves. He had a firm handshake. I told him my name. He told me his was "Kennesaw, like the mountain." What a perfect name, I thought. Soon we parted ways. I still reflect on Kennesaw whenever I ride through. I hope he's still feeding the crows, wherever he is.

As I rode off, I again thought about just how danged lucky I am. How else would I have found myself sitting on a picnic table in a park so far removed from my workaday life; how else would I ever have had the privilege to meet such an interesting person if I weren't a motorcyclist? Motorcyclists are blessed in this way!

Continue into Damascus, Virginia. Damascus is a cool little town along the southwestern State Line. Folks here fancy themselves having an outdoor town and for good reason. The Appalachian Trail comes through Damascus. It's the first significant town along the 2190-mile-long trail where hikers can purchase a needed shower and a bunk for a night or two off the ground, and where they can also re-provision themselves for the interminable trek farther north. There is at least one first-rate outfitter store in town to check out and several decent restaurants as well.

Damascus is also the home of the Virginia Creeper Trail. That's right! It's a rails-to-trails experience that's fun for the whole family! There are several shuttle companies that take riders and their own bicycles or rentals to the southern terminus of the trail, its highest point. Once they push off, they can coast all 17 miles back into town without having to pedal once. My wife and I have done the trail, and I didn't pedal at all!

Follow Route 58 roughly 34 miles back to Volney; it's about the best stretch of motorcycle road I've yet to find. You'll be treated to many sections of clean pavement, on-camber, low-gear curves. Beautiful scenery abounds, and if you want to ride into Grayson Highlands State Park to see the wild ponies, be my guest. Again, just don't stay long because, to quote the Robert Frost poem, there are still "miles to go" before you sleep.

Turn left at Volney onto Route 16. Ride 3.1 miles. Turn right onto Route 658. But before you do, stop in at the Fox Creek General Store right there on the corner. If it's still owned by Sarah, you're in luck! Sarah's an intrepid transplant from up North who has settled here. With gumption, cooking skills and a can-do attitude, she's created a most welcoming store for her wide-ranging clientele. She's made a genuine success of the place.

Now hear this! The combination of Flat Ridge Road, Fox Creek Road, Route 58, Old Bridle Creek Road, and Comers Rock Road is my nomination for the finest 35-mile combination of roads found anywhere in Virginia, if not the entire Untied States. If you don't believe me, just come here and ride what I am about to describe and judge for yourself! The entire stretch is a rolling picture postcard of smooth pavement and challenging curves. Riding these roads totally typifies the best of Appalachian Mountain riding. It's a lively romp through and through.

From the Fox Creek General Store, ride Rt. 658 (Flat Ridge Rd.) 4.8 miles. Bear right onto Fox Creek Road. Ride Fox Creek Rd, trending downhill, about 5 miles. Turn left onto Route 58. Ride 3.6 miles. Turn left onto Old Bridle Creek Road and trend back uphill 6.7 miles. Sweet! Now turn right and you're back on Rt. 658, only now it's called Comers Rock Rd. Ride nearly 16 miles to Route 21. There is a gas station on the right. It's a good place for a bio break after digesting Sarah's good cooking!

Turn north onto Route 21. Ride 8 miles to Speedwell, then turn right onto Route 619. Carefully ride Rt. 619. There is at least one left turn that's easy to miss. Continue 12.4 miles until you reach the main road at Route 94. Cross it and continue straight another 4.2 miles. Cross the New River and head into Austinville, Virginia, the hometown of Stephen Austin, "the Father of Texas." Just after you cross the bridge, there's a monument to Austin on the left.

Continue following the flow of the road until just before the interstate. There's a large truck stop on the left. I usually stop for one last break before the final push to Floyd, Virginia.

Turn left out of the large parking area back onto Rt. 619. Turn right onto Route 52.

You're going to ride Rt. 52 exactly 8.2 miles into the outskirts of Hillsville, VA. Turn onto Beaver Dam Road, a side street. That way, you'll circumvent all the honky-tonk of Hillsville. Ride 1.9 miles. Turn left onto Route 100, a main highway. Ride 1.2 miles. Turn right onto Buckhorn Road. Wend around on Buckhorn Road three miles and merge onto Double Cabin Road.

This is the final push to Floyd, where you will be spending the night. It should be getting on toward late afternoon by now. Once you get to Route 221, you could turn left and beeline to Floyd. But don't! Look around. The sunlight should be behind you and not in your eyes. The lighting should be excellent. I know it's late in the day and you're likely tired. But I want you to experience the "full plate." I want to share with you why the Appalachians are king! I want you to have a majestic experience, something you'll remember for years to come. You might even have your camera at the ready. We're headed back up to the Crest of the Blue Ridge and its fabulous Parkway at dusk for one more go — but allow me to digress for a moment with a quick recommendation: When I am feeling drowsy late in the afternoon, this is what I do to blow out "cobwebs" and restore myself to "AM" condition. I take a 100 milligram caffeine pill with a long tall slug of cool water. That's right! A 100 milligram pill is equal to a strong cup of dark roast in tablet form without the diuretic effect of coffee. I follow it with an analgesic of choice and pretty soon it feels like 9 AM. Just like that, I cover three necessities for safe motorcycling late in the day: I'm soon to be more alert, not as achey and more relaxed, and better hydrated than I was before.

Motor along Double Cabin Rd. 7.6 miles. Turn left onto Route 221. Ride 6.4 miles back into Willis and once again bear right on Conner Grove Road. Ride back up to Blue Ridge Plateau and the Parkway.

The Blue Ridge Plateau is a fascinating geological feature. The Plateau runs roughly 70 miles east-west along a stretch of the Blue Ridge Mountain from Bent Mountain just south of Roanoke to Interstate 77 at Fancy Gap, Virginia. The Plateau is on an angle. Its high side is the Blue Ridge Parkway. From all along it, the Plateau gradually slopes to the north downhill roughly 30 miles to the New River. 70 miles by 30 miles is a lot of square miles! In between are some of the finest technical motorcycle roads found anywhere on the planet. Anchoring the middle of the Plateau is Buffalo Mountain.

Since "the Buffalo," or just "the Buff" as it's called by the locals, is such a prominent feature in this region, let's have a good look at it. Ride to Milepost 168 and turn right and up a short hill to "The Saddle" overlook. Off in the distance you will see "the Buffalo." It's an ancient mountain shaped by the forces of nature into a buffalo's hump. The historical marker explains that mothers allowed their adolescent, foraging sons free range of the territory as long as they could see "the Buff" over their shoulders Isn't that cool? I've flown my Grumman Tiger over these parts several times and have purposely reconnoitered the Blue Ridge Plateau from the air to confirm my impressions of it. From 100 miles out, I could always make out "the Buffalo." It's a distinctive landmark with a storied history, and now you are a small part of that history, too. It is also the centerpiece of a Nature Conservancy preserve. The two-mile trail to the top provides an outstanding 360-degree view of the Plateau.

Living in the Greater Washington, DC area, and before I took the time to learn the roads here, I used to make the journey to the Asheville area at least once a year. Recently not so much. I've come to appreciate the hospitality, the sights and the roads along the Blue Ridge Plateau to the extent that I skip that now excessively popular destination. I save a few commuting days and still get my fill of beautiful scenery and great twisties by riding no farther than the Plateau and its surroundings. Getting to know its people has been a pleasure as well.

Speaking about great people, continue north on the Parkway and exit onto Route 8. Turn toward Floyd. Ride 5.8 miles into Floyd and turn right at the stoplight onto Route 221. Ride out of town 1.7 miles and turn left into the Pine Tavern. There you'll meet its accommodating innkeepers, Robin and David. If you become members of the "Red Chair Society," you'll sit out by the fire pit with a several-fingered glass (Members share a little class: No plastic cups in the "Red Chair Society!") of your favorite beverage and David will regale you with stories of his halcyon days as a rumbling bass player in the orbit of Stephen Stills, Jackson Browne, and Joni Mitchell. If you're there on a weekend, the Tavern's restaurant is open. If not, it's a short ride back into town where you can get a good meal at several restaurants.

Total miles for Day Seven: Approximately 355. That's a strong day of mountain riding by any measure!

Day Eight: The Gap Attack

One of the more interesting rides in and around the Blue Ridge Plateau is a crafted route called the "Gap Attack." It was shared with me by Will Beers one night over beers at Willville. This route will have you motoring up and down the steep southern slopes of the Plateau in a specific sequence. In other words, you want to be motoring uphill and not downhill on several of the gaps to maximize the grins. Begin your day over breakfast at Mabry Mill. You can't miss it — it's the most photographed sight on the entire Parkway, and their homemade pancakes are excellent.

The Art of Riding Smooth

After breakfast, ride north 17.1 miles and exit sharp to the right onto Shooting Creek Road. This is a deeply shaded invisible road that will get you 6.3 miles down the grade to the southern base of the Plateau. Turn right onto Route 40 and ride it 11 miles to Woolwine.

Route 40 is a sleeper and often ignored by riders for no reason other than they just don't know better. If you can somehow work it in, Route 40 from Woolwine to Ferrum is one of the finest stretches of pavement around. This piece of road is distinguished by having several sections of low-gear curves, on-camber beauties that are plain fun to ride.

From Woolwine, turn right on Route 8 and head 6.6 miles back up the grade to the Parkway. Near the very top, you'll ride past Tuggle Gap Restaurant and Motel. This is great place to hang out. Sherry, originally from California, purchased it from her mother a few years ago and has developed it into one of the more successful establishments along this region of the Parkway. You might stop there for lunch.

Turn south on the Parkway and exit into Meadows of Dan, eastbound on Route 58 and head back down the Plateau using all the same roads you used on your Southern Route to Pisgah. Exit again onto Rt. 58-Bus and make your way to and through Stuart by again turning right at the stoplight onto Main Street. If you didn't stop at the Honduras Coffee Shop earlier, this would probably be a good time of day to do so. Follow the flow of the road back onto Dobyns Road which, as you know, flows into Little Dan River Road on out to Route 103. From Tuggle's Gap and the Parkway to Rt. 103, this stretch is 38.7 miles long.

Turn right again onto Rt. 103. Ride 0.6 miles and turn again onto Ararat Road. Only this time, ride 1.6 miles and turn right onto Kibler Valley Road. You're actually riding into a box canyon with one way in and the same way out.

After a couple miles, the road does turn to dirt, but is smoothly graded so touring bikes and cruisers shouldn't have difficulty. Ride all 6.2 miles to where the road dead-ends. You'll find a power plant there as well as a restroom. This is also where the Dan River comes roaring out from somewhere within the mountain. Once you've checked out the place, return the same 6.2 miles to Ararat Road. Turn right.

Ride 12.3 miles. Keep your eyes peeled for Crossingham Road. Turn right. Crossingham Rd. is going to flow into Wards Gap Road. Continue 3.2 miles and bear left onto Fish Lake Road. Follow the flow of Fish Lake Road left onto Epworth Road and follow it 2.6 miles to Route 52, a main road. If somehow you get tangled up, just find Route 52.

Turn right. Ride 3 miles. Turn left onto Route 691/AKA Flower Gap Road. Flower Gap Rd. is a favorite 4.3-mile stretch of nice pavement with pretty vistas and is satisfying to ride. Turn right onto Old Pipers Gap Road. At the I-77 exchange, there's a large truck stop for a bio break. Take it!

Continue up Old Pipers Gap, which at some point will flow into Route 620/AKA Lambsburg Road. It's beautiful through here. You'll see! Notice the unusual deep forest scenery. From Flower Gap Rd., follow this combination of roads up the southern flanks of the Plateau 5.4 miles to the stop sign. Turn right on Route 775 (Chances Creek Road). Ride 7.3 miles. Turn right onto Route 52. Ride about a mile, but just before going underneath the Parkway overpass, there will be a nondescript restaurant on the right called the Lakeview Restaurant. Check it out. It's real good Southern home cooking and hospitality!

From the restaurant, continue south on Rt. 52 back down the Plateau. Ride 4.1 miles. Keep your eye peeled for Route 691/AKA Bear Trail Road. Turn left. Again, this is another superb invisible road with the Plateau now off to your left. Ride this baby 5.5 miles. You'll come to a stop sign. Turn right at Wards Gap Road and continue a short half-mile. At the T-intersection, turn left a sharp 120 degree onto Orchard Gap Rd. You're now going to boogie back up the Plateau 3 miles. Careful! There are several tight, low-gear curves as you make the climb. Don't stumble! Up top just before the Parkway, on the left, there's a convenience store for a break.

Turn north on the Parkway. Ride 1.5 miles. Turn right onto Willis Gap Road and back down you go! Ride 3.4 miles. Turn left onto Friends Mission Road. Follow the flow of this road as it winds along nearly 5 miles to Ararat Road. Turn left again and follow it

2.3 miles back to Squirrel Spur Road. Turn left yet again and motor 5.3 miles back up the mountain. You're almost "home!" Toward the top, at the fork in the road, fork right this time and remain on Squirrel Spur Rd. Ride 3.7 miles and turn left onto Mayberry Creek Road.

Mayberry Creek Rd. is a small detour that I want you to take so you can see the smallest of six fieldstone churches that were built back in the 1920s throughout the Blue Ridge Plateau by the Rev. Robert Childress. There's a long story about Rev. Childress and even a book ("The Man Who Moved A Mountain") written about him. He's revered in these parts. The book chronicles his efforts to organize and bring a semblance of peace to the mountain people of that period. The Blue Ridge Plateau was the last region along the crest of the Blue Ridge to receive and benefit from roads and education. By getting these hardscrabble mountain people to agree on building the churches, Childress was able to indirectly establish these two civic necessities, along with the Word of God, to the people living here who, beforehand, were more versed in the primal "Hatfield vs. McCoy" pursuits of stilling moonshine, alcoholism, murder, and revenge. The minster of this small church is the grandson of the elder Rev. Childress.

This detour will wind you around and back to Squirrel Spur Rd. Turn left and continue two miles back to the Poor Farmer's Market in Meadows of Dan for ice cream! Have a double... you deserve it!

Total miles for the Day Eight: Approximately 171 (and you didn't get out of your middle gears for most of it).

For your last night, you have a final hotel to consider. It's called Hotel Floyd and is located in downtown Floyd, VA. Try to stay in the old wing. It has more appeal and character than the new wing. Several restaurants will be within walking distance.

There you have it! In one volume you have the skills you can use to develop yourself into the expert street rider I hope you become, and a full-bore mountain ride to practice on. I hope you've enjoyed reading the book as much as I've enjoyed "riding" it!

See you in the right gear!

Jim Ford

February 2017

Finally allow me to indulge myself in a bit of shameless self-promotion. Go to my website at www.ridersworkshop.com. There you can purchase and download the gps file, hard copy maps, and a turn-by-turn description for the entire route.

If you care for in depth training on the finer points of the book, you can also sign on for one of my Appalachian tours/workshops. Like I wrote at the beginning you'll benefit from organized knowledge, structured supervision, and develop good habits. You'll also meet like minded riders and kindred spirits and have one hell of a good time too! Be sure to read the reviews. Riders who have attended my Workshop mostly say their experience exceeded their expectations. I'll strive to exceed your expectations too!

About the Author

Jim Ford lives in Kensington, Maryland with Annie Hayes, his soulmate of 25 years, and their Wonder Dog, Zen.

Jim trained in the Cessna 172 and earned his pilot's license in 1989. He owned a Grumman AA5-B Tiger for eight years and flew it 1500 hours.

Jim started motorcycling in 1992 and sold motorcycles for Bob's BMW in Jessup, Maryland from 1996 to 2004. Since 1992, he has ridden nearly 600,000 miles, over 98% of which has been within the Appalachian Mountains. He created The Rider's Workshop LLC in 2006.

His license plate is: Zen.

www.ridersworkshop.com
jim@ridersworkshop.com
301-520-1649

Made in the USA
Lexington, KY
01 February 2018